Tulips &
Chimneys

By E. E. Cummings
In Liveright paperback

The Enormous Room

Etcetera

is 5

No Thanks

Selected Poems

Tulips & Chimneys

22 and 50 Poems

ViVa

XAIPE

In Liveright clothbound

Complete Poems 1904–1962

Tulips & Chimneys

E. E. CUMMINGS

LIVERIGHT

New York   London

Reissued in Liveright paperback 1996

Manufacturing by RR Donnelley Westford

Library of Congress Cataloging in Publication Data

Cummings, Edward Estlin, 1894–1962.
Tulips & chimneys.

I. Title.
PS3505.U334T8   1976   811'.5'2   76-10204

ISBN 0-87140-165-7

Liveright Publishing Corporation
500 Fifth Avenue, N.Y., N.Y. 10110

W. W. Norton & Company Ltd.
Castle House, 75/76 Wells Street, London W1T 3QT

Printed in the United States of America

4 5 6 7 8 9 0

CONTENTS

CHIMNEYS

& [AND] (1925)

A

POST IMPRESSIONS

INTRODUCTION
by
Richard S. Kennedy

More than half a century has passed since E. E. Cummings put together a remarkable collection of poems entitled *Tulips & Chimneys* in 1919; and incredible as it must seem, only now can the general reader see this collection in its author's own arrangement of the contents and experience its full impact. Some of his friends, like Stewart Mitchell, John Dos Passos, and John Peale Bishop, did have the privilege of reading through that manuscript or through the final, 1922 version. But the rest of us have had to wait until now to see what a bedazzling display of poetic talent the completed manuscript contained—a manuscript that no publisher was willing to take a chance on in the early 1920's. The story of what happened to *Tulips & Chimneys* clearly reveals the conservatism of the American literary scene just after World War I, a conservatism that Cummings was eager to put to rout.

After three years and many rejections (even by Liveright, who issued his war narrative, *The Enormous Room,* in 1922), Cummings had almost lost hope of getting his "bookofpoems" into print when John Dos Passos persuaded Thomas Seltzer to publish a volume of selections from the manuscript. Seltzer gingerly avoided the most experimental of the poems and tried to pass over those whose subject matter might startle readers who were still unwilling to accept the work of Carl Sandburg or Theodore Dreiser. The result was a book entitled *Tulips and Chimneys* that contained only 66 of the 152 poems in the manuscript. It was published in 1923.

Early the following year, the Dial Press was given the opportunity to publish the rest of the poems; but its editor, Lincoln MacVeagh, tiptoed past such dangers as "between the breasts" and "my naked lady framed" and decided to publish another volume of selections, *XLI Poems*. This was issued in 1925. "When my beard is white with dotage, etc.," Cummings wrote to his mother, "the entire *Tulips & Chimneys* may possibly have made an appearance per 71 different selective passages conducted by 407 publishers."[1]

Shortly after MacVeagh had made his choice, Cummings arranged to have the 45 remaining poems printed privately. He was happy to discover that the unselected poems constituted his "most personal work,"[2] a reference perhaps to the many sonnets he had written for his first wife, Elaine Orr, to whom he dedicated the volume. This book, entitled *&*, also appeared in 1925 and contained 34 additional poems which are now included in the present edition. Almost all of them had been written before 1920 and more than half of them had been part of the original, 1919 version of the manuscript. When Cummings revised and rearranged *Tulips & Chimneys* in 1922, he omitted some of the poems in this group probably because he thought they would scare off publishers who were unwilling to do battle with such self-appointed guardians of public morals as John S. Sumner, executive secretary of the New York Society for the Suppression of Vice. With a privately printed edition there would be no problems about prosecution.

Cummings had another reason for remembering 1925, for in that year he was chosen to receive the coveted Dial Award for "distinguished service to American letters." The Award was a money prize of $2000, enough in those days for a poet to live on for a year (and for the frugal Cummings to live on for two years). The money was helpful to a man who was determined to live by means of his writing; but the fame was what counted most. What would that recognition have meant to Cummings if he had found a publisher for his manuscript in 1920? What would the impact have been on American letters if his poems had been published all together, stylistically reinforcing each other? His career as a poet would certainly have been fully launched when he was still only twenty-six years old; and the healthy influence of his unique style would have been felt five years earlier (two years before *The Waste Land*) and would have helped to take a hitch in the cultural lag of the American literary scene of that time.

But even so, Cummings' own development probably would have taken the same general course. He would still have been a poet and a painter and an individualist and an iconoclast, for his heritage and early upbringing gave him his special kind of talent and personality. Edward Estlin Cummings was born October 14, 1894, and brought up in Cambridge, Massachusetts, in a home that was only a two-minute walk from the Harvard Yard. He was the son of Edward Cummings, who became one of the leading Unitarian ministers of Boston, and Rebecca Haswell Clarke, who was descended from ancestors with literary and intellectual leanings going back as far as Susanna Haswell Rowson, the author of *Charlotte Temple*, the first American novel. His mother encouraged him from an early age to draw and sketch and to write verses. After preparing for college at the Cambridge Latin School, Cummings entered Harvard in 1911 and concentrated in classics. He was graduated with an A.B., *magna cum laude*, in Greek and English literature, in 1915 and remained to take a Master's degree in English in 1916. During these years he published many conventional poems in *The Harvard Monthly* and, on occasion, in its rival, *The Harvard Advocate.* He also contributed to a respectable anthology, *Eight Harvard Poets,* and associated with a literary group of friends who later made *The Dial* the most distinguished magazine of the arts in America in the 1920s.

While at Harvard, Cummings became intensely interested in the new movements in the visual arts: Impressionism, Cézanne and Post-Impressionism, Cubism, and Futurism. He read the new poets—Pound, H.D., Sandburg, and Amy Lowell—and started to write free verse and to follow the Imagist principles laid down by Pound: to use the rhythms of common speech rather than metrical regularity; to strive for compression and precision in language; to avoid worn-out poetic diction; and to make poetic statement by means of images. Full of creative fervor and seeking fresh and unusual effects, he began, by 1916, to create a style of his own.

"The symbol of all art is the Prism," he later noted in a series of critical dicta. "The goal is unrealism. The method is destructive. To break up the white light of objective realism, into the secret glories which it contains."[3] He tried out his own form of literary Cubism, breaking up his material and presenting it in a new, visually directive way upon the page. But this period of experimentation was interrupted, in 1917, when the United States entered the war in Europe, and Cummings, although he was basically a pacifist, volunteered for service in the Norton-Harjes Ambulance Corps. Not long after he took up his duties in France, some indiscreet letters written by a fellow volunteer and close friend, plus his own effervescence, lack of discipline, and open espousal of the pacifist position, landed the poet and his companion in a French concentration camp for three months under suspicion of espionage. This experience formed the basis of his book, *The Enormous Room.* Back in the States after his release, he was once again painting and writing in

New York, activities which did not cease even when he was drafted into the Army for a short tour of duty which he spent at Camp Devens, Massachusetts.

By the time Cummings returned to civilian life in January 1919, he had begun to exhibit a distinctive poetic style, one which established its own grammatical usages, its own punctuation, and its own rules for capitalization in the freest kind of verse. This linguistic exuberance was not the result of any inability to express himself in controlled verse forms: he could turn out a traditional sonnet in half an hour. But even in this hallowed form he broke with tradition. He wandered far from the accepted kind of subject matter and wrote sonnets which recorded the gurgle of wash basins, the click of billiard balls, and lustful tumblings on rumpled beds.

Throughout this period Cummings sent one batch of poems after another to magazines, but he could not get them published. Undaunted, he decided to compile a book-length volume. From the hundreds of poems he had written, he selected a body of work that represented a wide variety of his verse and also displayed his movement away from traditional forms and his gradual achievement of an analytical style.

In 1920, when his poems began to appear in *The Dial*, and again in 1923, when Thomas Seltzer issued the truncated version of *Tulips & Chimneys*, the initial response of the reading public was to the superficial features of Cummings' style—the free play with punctuation and the scattering of words on the page. Even as open-minded a critic of the avant-garde as Edmund Wilson was taken aback by the "eccentric punctuation" and unconventional visual arrangements. He lodged his complaint this way:

> But the really serious case against Mr. Cummings's punctuation is that the results which it yields are ugly. His poems on the page are hid-

eous. He insists on breaking up even the least un-
conventional of his verses which would be more
appropriately printed as neat little blocks of type
like the prose poems of Logan Pearsall Smith, into
systems of exploded fragments, and this, so far
from making the cadences plainer, only involves us
in a jigsaw puzzle of putting the lines together
again.[4]

Like Joyce, Eliot, Faulkner, and other literary innovators,
Cummings gradually taught his audience how to read his
work; and with Pound and others he carried *vers libre* into
visually directive forms. The appearance of almost any page
in an anthology of present-day poetry owes something to the
flexibility that Cummings introduced into American verse.

Many individual poems in *Tulips & Chimneys* are worth
close analysis, but what is most important is the delight we
can take in just browsing through the whole collection and
getting to know the engaging personality of the artist who
performs for us here. For the poems comment on each
other, and the accumulative experience teaches us how to
read them, adapting ourselves as we go along to the poet's
idiom. We can also witness the development of Cummings'
unique poetic talent, from the workshop pieces of his college
days and the early literary experiments to the first of his
achievements as a true "draughtsman of words."

Only one thing is missing, something which is quite evi-
dent in Cummings' later publications. Since *Tulips & Chim-
neys* is his first book of verse, the very heterogeneity which
gives it its special interest obscures that clear sense of an
outlook on life which is distinctive in Cummings' career as
an American poet. His later volumes have that center—a
simple, coherent view which is implied only in a scattering
of the poems in this volume. That view is an affirmation of

life in all its multiplicity, but especially in whatever is simple, natural, individual, unique. It is a rejection of social forces which hinder the expression of that uniqueness, especially those forces which promote groupiness, conformity, imitation, artificiality. It values whatever is instinctively human, especially feeling and imagination. It is willing to jettison the products, both tangible and psychic, of our overorganized, emotionally anaesthetized, technologically quantified civilization.

In the early 1920s, E. E. Cummings had only started on his way to that view of life, but he had already achieved a personal style in which to express it. It is our pleasure to see in *Tulips & Chimneys* the emergence of that style and to realize that, because of it, American poetry would never be the same again.

Temple University
Philadelphia, Pennsylvania
June 1976

NOTES

1. Unpublished letter, May 26, 1924, in The Houghton Library, Harvard University.
2. Unpublished letter to S. A. Jacobs, Spring 1924, in the Clifton Waller Barrett Library, University of Virginia Library.
3. Unpublished notes, The Houghton Library.
4. Review of *Tulips & Chimneys, New Republic*, March 19, 1924.

TULIPS

EPITHALAMION

I.

Thou aged unreluctant earth who dost
with quivering continual thighs invite
the thrilling rain the slender paramour
to toy with thy extraordinary lust,
(the sinuous rain which rising from thy bed
steals to his wife the sky and hour by hour
wholly renews her pale flesh with delight)
—immortally whence are the high gods fled?

Speak elm eloquent pandar with thy nod
significant to the ecstatic earth
in token of his coming whom her soul
burns to embrace—and didst thou know the god
from but the imprint of whose cloven feet
the shrieking dryad sought her leafy goal,
at the mere echo of whose shining mirth
the furious hearts of mountains ceased to beat?

Wind beautifully who wanderest
over smooth pages of forgotten joy
proving the peaceful theorems of the flowers
—didst e'er depart upon more exquisite quest?
and did thy fortunate fingers sometime dwell
(within a greener shadow of secret bowers)
among the curves of that delicious boy
whose serious grace one goddess loved too well?

Chryselephantine Zeus Olympian
sceptred colossus of the Pheidian soul
whose eagle frights creation,in whose palm
Nike presents the crown sweetest to man,

whose lilied robe the sun's white hands emboss,
betwixt whose absolute feet anoint with calm
of intent stars circling the acerb pole
poises,smiling,the diadumenos

in whose young chiseled eyes the people saw
their once again victorious Pantarkes
(whose grace the prince of artists made him bold
to imitate between the feet of awe),
thunderer whose omnipotent brow showers
its curls of unendured eternal gold
over the infinite breast in bright degrees,
whose pillow is the graces and the hours,

father of gods and men whose subtle throne
twain sphinxes bear each with a writhing youth
caught to her brazen breasts,whose foot-stool tells
how fought the looser of the warlike zone
of her that brought forth tall Hippolytus,
lord on whose pedestal the deep expels
(over Selene's car closing uncouth)
of Helios the sweet wheels tremulous—

are there no kings in Argos,that the song
is silent,of the steep unspeaking tower
within whose brightening strictness Danae
saw the night severed and the glowing throng
descend,felt on her flesh the amorous strain
of gradual hands and yielding to that fee
her eager body's unimmortal flower
knew in the darkness a more burning rain?

2.

And still the mad magnificent herald Spring
assembles beauty from forgetfulness
with the wild trump of April:witchery
of sound and odour drives the wingless thing

man forth into bright air,for now the red
leaps in the maple's cheek,and suddenly
by shining hordes in sweet unserious dress
ascends the golden crocus from the dead.

On dappled dawn forth rides the pungent sun
with hooded day preening upon his hand
followed by gay untimid final flowers
(which dressed in various tremulous armor stun
the eyes of ragged earth who sees them pass)
while hunted from his kingdom winter cowers,
seeing green armies steadily expand
hearing the spear-song of the marching grass.

A silver sudden parody of snow
tickles the air to golden tears,and hark!
the flicker's laughing yet,while on the hills
the pines deepen to whispers primeval and throw
backward their foreheads to the barbarous bright
sky,and suddenly from the valley thrills
the unimaginable upward lark
and drowns the earth and passes into light

(slowly in life's serene perpetual round
a pale world gathers comfort to her soul,
hope richly scattered by the abundant sun
invades the new mosaic of the ground
—let but the incurious curtaining dusk be drawn
surpassing nets are sedulously spun
to snare the brutal dew,—the authentic scroll
of fairie hands and vanishing with dawn).

Spring,that omits no mention of desire
in every curved and curling thing,yet holds
continuous intercourse—through skies and trees
the lilac's smoke the poppy's pompous fire
the pansy's purple patience and the grave
frailty of daises—by what rare unease

revealed of teasingly transparent folds—
with man's poor soul superlatively brave.

Surely from robes of particoloured peace
with mouth flower-faint and undiscovered eyes
and dim slow perfect body amorous
(whiter than lilies which are born and cease
for being whiter than this world)exhales
the hovering high perfume curious
of that one month for whom the whole year dies,
risen at length from palpitating veils.

O still miraculous May!O shining girl
of time untarnished!O small intimate
gently primeval hands,frivolous feet
divine!O singular and breathless pearl!
O indefinable frail ultimate pose!
O visible beatitude sweet sweet
intolerable!silence immaculate
of god's evasive audible great rose!

3.

Lover,lead forth thy love unto that bed
prepared by whitest hands of waiting years,
curtained with wordless worship absolute,
unto the certain altar at whose head
stands that clear candle whose expecting breath
exults upon the tongue of flame half-mute,
(haste ere some thrush with silver several tears
complete the perfumed paraphrase of death).

Now is the time when all occasional things
close into silence,only one tree,one
svelte translation of eternity
unto the pale meaning of heaven clings,

(whose million leaves in winsome indolence
simmer upon thinking twilight momently)
as down the oblivious west's numerous dun
magnificence conquers magnificence.

In heaven's intolerable athanor
inimitably tortured the base day
utters at length her soft intrinsic hour,
and from those tenuous fires which more and more
sink and are lost the divine alchemist,
the magus of creation,lifts a flower—
whence is the world's insufferable clay
clothed with incognizable amethyst.

Lady at whose imperishable smile
the amazed doves flicker upon sunny wings
as if in terror of eternity,
(or seeming that they would mistrust a while
the moving of beauteous dead mouths throughout
that very proud transparent company
of quivering ghosts-of-love which scarcely sings
drifting in slow diaphanous faint rout),

queen in the inconceivable embrace
of whose tremendous hair that blossom stands
whereof is most desire,yet less than those
twain perfect roses whose ambrosial grace,
goddess,thy crippled thunder-forging groom
or the loud lord of skipping maenads knows,—
having Discordia's apple in thy hands,
which the scared shepherd gave thee for his doom—

O thou within the chancel of whose charms
the tall boy god of everlasting war
received the shuddering sacrament of sleep,
betwixt whose cool incorrigible arms
impaled upon delicious mystery,
with gaunt limbs reeking of the whispered deep,

deliberate groping ocean fondled o'er
the warm long flower of unchastity,

imperial Cytherea,from frail foam
sprung with irrevocable nakedness
to strike the young world into smoking song—
as the first star perfects the sensual dome
of darkness,and the sweet strong final bird
transcends the sight,O thou to whom belong
the hearts of lovers!—I beseech thee bless
thy suppliant singer and his wandering word.

OF NICOLETTE

dreaming in marble all the castle lay
like some gigantic ghost-flower born of night
blossoming in white towers to the moon,
soft sighed the passionate darkness to the tune
of tiny troubadours,and(phantom-white)
dumb-blooming boughs let fall their glorious snows,
and the unearthly sweetness of a rose
swam upward from the troubled heart of May;

a Winged Passion woke and one by one
there fell upon the night,like angel's tears,
the syllables of that mysterious prayer,
and as an opening lily drowsy-fair
(when from her couch of poppy petals peers
the sleepy morning)gently draws apart
her curtains,and lays bare her trembling heart,
with beads of dew made jewels by the sun,

so one high shining tower(which as a glass
turned light to flame and blazed with snowy fire)
unfolding,gave the moon a nymphlike face,

a form whose snowy symmetry of grace
haunted the limbs as music haunts the lyre,
a creature of white hands,who letting fall
a thread of lustre from the castle wall
glided,a drop of radiance,to the grass—

shunning the sudden moonbeam's treacherous snare
she sought the harbouring dark,and(catching up
her delicate silk)all white,with shining feet,
went forth into the dew:right wildly beat
her heart at every kiss of daisy-cup,
and from her cheek the beauteous colour went
with every bough that reverently bent
to touch the yellow wonder of her hair.

SONGS

I

(thee will i praise between those rivers whose
white voices pass upon forgetting(fail
me not)whose courseless waters are a gloat
of silver;o'er whose night three willows wail,
a slender dimness in the unshapeful hour
making dear moan in tones of stroked flower;
let not thy lust one threaded moment lose:
haste)the very shadowy sheep float
free upon terrific pastures pale,

whose tall mysterious shepherd lifts a cheek
teartroubled to the momentary wind
with guiding smile,lips wisely minced for blown
kisses,condemnatory fingers thinned
of pity—so he stands counting the moved
myriads wonderfully loved,

(hasten,it is the moment which shall seek
all blossoms that do learn,scents of not known
musics in whose careful eyes are dinned;

and the people of perfect darkness fills
his mind who will their hungering whispers hear
with weepings soundless,saying of "alas
we were chaste on earth we ghosts:hark to the sheer
cadence of our grey flesh in the gloom!
and still to be immortal is our doom;
but a rain frailly raging whom the hills
sink into and their sunsets,it shall pass.
Our feet tread sleepless meadows sweet with fear")

then be with me:unseriously seem
by the perusing greenness of thy thought
my golden soul fabulously to glue
in a superior terror;be thy taut
flesh silver,like the currency of faint
cities eternal—ere the sinless taint
of thy long sinful arms about me dream
shall my love wholly taste thee as a new
wine from steep hills by darkness softly brought—

(be with me in the sacred witchery
of almostness which May makes follow soon
on the sweet heels of passed afterday,
clothe thy soul's coming merely,with a croon
of mingling robes musically revealed
in rareness:let thy twain eyes deeply wield
a noise of petals falling silently
through the far-spaced possible nearaway
from huge trees drenched by a rounding moon)

II

when life is quite through with
and leaves say alas,
much is to do
for the swallow,that closes
a flight in the blue;

when love's had his tears out,
perhaps shall pass
a million years
(while a bee dozes
on the poppies,the dears;

when all's done and said,and
under the grass
lies her head
by oaks and roses
deliberated.)

III

Always before your voice my soul
half-beautiful and wholly droll
is as some smooth and awkward foal,
whereof young moons begin
the newness of his skin,

so of my stupid sincere youth
the exquisite failure uncouth
discovers a trembling and smooth
Unstrength,against the strong
silences of your song;

or as a single lamb whose sheen
of full unsheared fleece is mean
beside its lovelier friends,between
your thoughts more white than wool
My thought is sorrowful:

but my heart smote in trembling thirds
of anguish quivers to your words,
As to a flight of thirty birds
shakes with a thickening fright
the sudden fooled light.

it is the autumn of a year:
When through the thin air stooped with fear,
across the harvest whitely peer
empty of surprise
death's faultless eyes

(whose hand my folded soul shall know
while on faint hills do fraily go
The peaceful terrors of the snow,
and before your dead face
which sleeps,a dream shall pass)

and these my days their sounds and flowers
Fall in a pride of petaled hours,
like flowers at the feet of mowers
whose bodies strong with love
through meadows hugely move.

yet what am i that such and such
mysteries very simply touch
me,whose heart-wholeness overmuch
Expects of your hair pale,
a terror musical?

while in an earthless hour my fond
soul seriously yearns beyond

this fern of sunset frond on frond
opening in a rare
Slowness of gloried air...

The flute of morning stilled in noon—
noon the implacable bassoon—
now Twilight seeks the thrill of moon,
washed with a wild and thin
despair of violin

IV

Thy fingers make early flowers of
all things.
thy hair mostly the hours love:
a smoothness which
sings,saying
(though love be a day)
do not fear,we will go amaying.

thy whitest feet crisply are straying.
Always
thy moist eyes are at kisses playing,
whose strangeness much
says;singing
(though love be a day)
for which girl art thou flowers bringing?

To be thy lips is a sweet thing
and small.
Death,Thee i call rich beyond wishing
if this thou catch,
else missing.
(though love be a day
and life be nothing,it shall not stop kissing).

V

All in green went my love riding
on a great horse of gold
into the silver dawn.

four lean hounds crouched low and smiling
the merry deer ran before.

Fleeter be they than dappled dreams
the swift sweet deer
the red rare deer.

Four red roebuck at a white water
the cruel bugle sang before.

Horn at hip went my love riding
riding the echo down
into the silver dawn.

four lean hounds crouched low and smiling
the level meadows ran before.

Softer be they than slippered sleep
the lean lithe deer
the fleet flown deer.

Four fleet does at a gold valley
the famished arrow sang before.

Bow at belt went my love riding
riding the mountain down
into the silver dawn.

four lean hounds crouched low and smiling
the sheer peaks ran before.

Paler be they than daunting death
the sleek slim deer
the tall tense deer.

Four tall stags at a green mountain
the lucky hunter sang before.

All in green went my love riding
on a great horse of gold
into the silver dawn.

four lean hounds crouched low and smiling
my heart fell dead before.

VI

Where's Madge then,
Madge and her men?
buried with
Alice in her hair,
(but if you ask the rain
he'll not tell where.)

beauty makes terms
with time and his worms,
when loveliness
says sweetly Yes
to wind and cold;
and how much earth
is Madge worth?
Inquire of the flower that sways in the autumn
she will never guess.
but i know

VII

Doll's boy 's asleep
under a stile
he sees eight and twenty
ladies in a line

the first lady
says to nine ladies
his lips drink water
but his heart drinks wine

the tenth lady
says to nine ladies
they must chain his foot
for his wrist 's too fine

the nineteenth
says to nine ladies
you take his mouth
for his eyes are mine.

Doll's boy 's asleep
under the stile
for every mile the feet go
the heart goes nine

VIII

cruelly,love
walk the autumn long;
the last flower in whose hair,
thy lips are cold with songs

for which is
first to wither,to pass?
shallowness of sunlight
falls and,cruelly,
across the grass
Comes the
moon

love,walk the
autumn
love,for the last
flower in the hair withers;
thy hair is acold with
dreams,
love thou art frail

—walk the longness of autumn
smile dustily to the people,
for winter
who crookedly care.

IX

when god lets my body be

From each brave eye shall sprout a tree
fruit that dangles therefrom

the purpled world will dance upon
Between my lips which did sing

a rose shall beget the spring
that maidens whom passion wastes

will lay between their little breasts
My strong fingers beneath the snow

Into strenuous birds shall go
my love walking in the grass

their wings will touch with her face
and all the while shall my heart be

With the bulge and nuzzle of the sea

PUELLA MEA

Harun Omar and Master Hafiz
keep your dead beautiful ladies.
Mine is a little lovelier
than any of your ladies were.

In her perfectest array
my lady,moving in the day,
is a little stranger thing
than crisp Sheba with her king
in the morning wandering.
  Through the young and awkward hours
my lady perfectly moving,
through the new world scarce astir
my fragile lady wandering
in whose perishable poise
is the mystery of Spring
(with her beauty more than snow
dexterous and fugitive
my very frail lady drifting
distinctly,moving like a myth
in the uncertain morning,with

April feet like sudden flowers
and all her body filled with May)
—moving in the unskilful day
my lady utterly alive,
to me is a more curious thing
(a thing more nimble and complete)
than ever to Judea's king
were the shapely sharp cunning
and withal delirious feet
of the Princess Salomé
carefully dancing in the noise
of Herod's silence,long ago.

If she a little turn her head
i know that i am wholly dead:
nor ever did on such a throat
the lips of Tristram slowly dote,
La beale Isoud whose leman was.
And if my lady look at me
(with her eyes which like two elves
incredibly amuse themselves)
with a look of faerie,
perhaps a little suddenly
(as sometimes the improbable
beauty of my lady will)
—at her glance my spirit shies
rearing(as in the miracle
of a lady who had eyes
which the king's horses might not kill.)
    But should my lady smile,it were
a flower of so pure surprise
(it were so very new a flower,
a flower so frail,a flower so glad)
as trembling used to yield with dew
when the world was young and new
(a flower such as the world had
in Springtime when the world was mad

and Launcelot spoke to Guenever,
a flower which most heavy hung
with silence when the world was young
and Diarmuid looked in Grania's eyes.)
    But should my lady's beauty play
at not speaking(sometimes as
it will)the silence of her face
doth immediately make
in my heart so great a noise,
as in the sharp and thirsty blood
of Paris would not all the Troys
of Helen's beauty:never did
Lord Jason(in impossible things
victorious impossibly)
so wholly burn,to undertake
Medea's rescuing eyes;nor he
when swooned the white egyptian day
who with Egypt's body lay.

Lovely as those ladies were
mine is a little lovelier.

And if she speaks in her frail way,
it is wholly to bewitch
my smallest thought with a most swift
radiance wherein slowly drift
murmurous things divinely bright;
it is foolingly to smite
my spirit with the lithe free twitch
of scintillant space,with the cool writhe
of gloom truly which syncopate
some sunbeam's skilful fingerings;
it is utterly to lull
with foliate inscrutable
sweetness my soul obedient;
it is to stroke my being with
numbing forests frolicsome,

fleetly mystical,aroam
with keen creatures of idiom
(beings alert and innocent
very deftly upon which
indolent miracles impinge)
—it is distinctly to confute
my reason with the deep caress
of every most shy thing and mute,
it is to quell me with the twinge
of all living intense things.

    Never my soul so fortunate
is(past the luck of all dead men
and loving)as invisibly when
upon her palpable solitude
a furtive occult fragrance steals,
a gesture of immaculate
perfume—whereby(with fear aglow)
my soul is wont wholly to know
the poignant instantaneous fern
whose scrupulous enchanted fronds
toward all things intrinsic yearn,
the immanent subliminal
fern of her delicious voice
(of her voice which always dwells
beside the vivid magical
impetuous and utter ponds
of dream;and very secret food
its leaves inimitable find
beyond the white authentic springs,
beyond the sweet instinctive wells,
which make to flourish the minute
spontaneous meadow of her mind)
—the vocal fern,always which feels
the keen ecstatic actual tread
(and thereto perfectly responds)
of all things exquisite and dead,
all living things and beautiful.

(Caliph and king their ladies had
to love them and to make them glad,
when the world was young and mad,
in the city of Bagdad—
mine is a little lovelier
than any of those ladies were.)

Her body is most beauteous,
being for all things amorous
fashioned very curiously
of roses and of ivory.
The immaculate crisp head
is such as only certain dead
and careful painters love to use
for their youngest angels(whose
praising bodies in a row
between slow glories fleetly go.)
Upon a keen and lovely throat
the strangeness of her face doth float,
which in eyes and lips consists
—always upon the mouth there trysts
curvingly a fragile smile
which like a flower lieth(while
within the eyes is dimly heard
a wistful and precarious bird.)
Springing from fragrant shoulders small,
ardent,and perfectly withal
smooth to stroke and sweet to see
as a supple and young tree,
her slim lascivious arms alight
in skilful wrists which hint at flight
—my lady's very singular
and slenderest hands moreover are
(which as lilies smile and quail)
of all things perfect the most frail.

(Whoso rideth in the tale
of Chaucer knoweth many a pair
of companions blithe and fair;

who to walk with Master Gower
in Confessio doth prefer
shall not lack for beauty there,
nor he that will amaying go
with my lord Boccaccio—
whoso knocketh at the door
of Marie and of Maleore
findeth of ladies goodly store
whose beauty did in nothing err.
If to me there shall appear
than a rose more sweetly known,
more silently than a flower,
my lady naked in her hair—
i for those ladies nothing care
nor any lady dead and gone.)

Each tapering breast is firm and smooth
that in a lovely fashion doth
from my lady's body grow;
as morning may a lily know,
her petaled flesh doth entertain
the adroit blood's mysterious skein
(but like some passionate earlier
flower,the snow will oft utter,
whereof the year has perfect bliss—
for each breast a blossom is,
which being a little while caressed
its fragrance makes the lover blest.)
Her waist is a most tiny hinge
of flesh,a winsome thing and strange;
apt in my hand warmly to lie
it is a throbbing neck whereby
to grasp the belly's ample vase
(that urgent urn which doth amass
for whoso drinks,a dizzier wine
than should the grapes of heaven combine
with earth's madness)—'tis a gate
unto a palace intricate

(whereof the luscious pillars rise
which are her large and shapely thighs)
in whose dome the trembling bliss
of a kingdom wholly is.
    Beneath her thighs such legs are seen
as were the pride of the world's queen:
each is a verb,miraculous
inflected oral devious,
beneath the body's breathing noun
(moreover the delicious frown
of the grave great sensual knees
well might any monarch please.)
Each ankle is divinely shy;
as if for fear you would espy
the little distinct foot(if whose
very minuteness doth abuse
reason,why then the artificer
did most exquisitely err.)

When the world was like a song
heard behind a golden door,
poet and sage and caliph had
to love them and to make them glad
ladies with lithe eyes and long
(when the world was like a flower
Omar Hafiz and Harun
loved their ladies in the moon)
—fashioned very curiously
of roses and of ivory
if naked she appears to me
my flesh is an enchanted tree;
with her lips' most frail parting
my body hears the cry of Spring,
and with their frailest syllable
its leaves go crisp with miracle.

Love!—maker of my lady,
in that always beyond this

poem or any poem she
of whose body words are afraid
perfectly beautiful is,
forgive these words which i have made.
And never boast your dead beauties,
you greatest lovers in the world!
who with Grania strangely fled,
who with Egypt went to bed,
whom white-thighed Semiramis
put up her mouth to wholly kiss—
never boast your dead beauties,
mine being unto me sweeter
(of whose shy delicious glance
things which never more shall be,
perfect things of faerie,
are intense inhabitants;
in whose warm superlative
body do distinctly live
all sweet cities passed away—
in her flesh at break of day
are the smells of Nineveh,
in her eyes when day is gone
are the cries of Babylon.)
Diarmuid Paris and Solomon,
Omar Harun and Master Hafiz,
to me your ladies are all one—
keep your dead beautiful ladies.

Eater of all things lovely—Time!
upon whose watering lips the world
poises a moment(futile,proud,
a costly morsel of sweet tears)
gesticulates,and disappears—
of all dainties which do crowd
gaily upon oblivion
sweeter than any there is one;
to touch it is the fear of rhyme—
in life's very fragile hour

(when the world was like a tale
made of laughter and of dew,
was a flight,a flower,a flame,
was a tendril fleetly curled
upon frailness)used to stroll
(very slowly)one or two
ladies like flowers made,
softly used to wholly move
slender ladies made of dream
(in the lazy world and new
sweetly used to laugh and love
ladies with crisp eyes and frail,
in the city of Bagdad.)

Keep your dead beautiful ladies
Harun Omar and Master Hafiz.

CHANSONS INNOCENTES

I

in Just-
spring   when the world is mud-
luscious the little
lame balloonman

whistles   far   and wee

and eddieandbill come
running from marbles and
piracies and it's
spring

when the world is puddle-wonderful

the queer
old balloonman whistles
far   and   wee
and bettyandisbel come dancing

from hop-scotch and jump-rope and

it's
spring
and
    the

        goat-footed

balloonMan   whistles
far
and
wee

||

hist   whist
little ghostthings
tip-toe
twinkle-toe

little twitchy
witches and tingling
goblins
hob-a-nob   hob-a-nob

little hoppy happy
toad in tweeds
tweeds
little itchy mousies

with scuttling
eyes   rustle and run   and
hidehidehide
whisk

whisk   look out for the old woman
with the wart on her nose
what she'll do to yer
nobody knows

for she knows the devil   ooch
the devil   ouch
the devil
ach   the great

green
dancing
devil
devil

devil
devil

wheeEEE

III

little tree
little silent Christmas tree
you are so little
you are more like a flower

who found you in the green forest
and were you very sorry to come away?

see   i will comfort you
because you smell so sweetly

i will kiss your cool bark
and hug you safe and tight
just as your mother would,
only don't be afraid

look   the spangles
that sleep all the year in a dark box
dreaming of being taken out and allowed to shine,
the balls the chains red and gold the fluffy threads,

put up your little arms
and i'll give them all to you to hold
every finger shall have its ring
and there won't be a single place dark or unhappy

then when you're quite dressed
you'll stand in the window for everyone to see
and how they'll stare!
oh but you'll be very proud

and my little sister and i will take hands
and looking up at our beautiful tree
we'll dance and sing
"Noel Noel"

IV

why did you go
little fourpaws?
you forgot to shut
your big eyes.

where did you go?
like little kittens
are all the leaves
which open in the rain.

little kittens who
are called spring,
is what we stroke
maybe asleep?

do you know?or maybe did
something go away
ever so quietly
when we weren't looking.

V

Tumbling-hair
　　　　　picker of buttercups
　　　　　　　　　　　violets
dandelions
And the big bullying daisies
　　　　　　　　　　through the field wonderful
with eyes a little sorry
Another comes
　　　　　also picking flowers

ORIENTALE

I

i spoke to thee
with a smile and thou didst not
answer
thy mouth is as
a chord of crimson music
                              Come hither
O thou,is life not a smile?

i spoke to thee with
a song and thou
didst not listen
thine eyes are as a vase
of divine silence
                    Come hither
O thou,is life not a song?

i spoke
to thee with a soul and
thou didst not wonder
thy face is as a dream locked
in white fragrance
                         Come hither
O thou,is life not love?

i speak to
thee with a sword
and thou art silent
thy breast is as a tomb
softer than flowers
                         Come hither
O thou,is love not death?

II

my love
thy hair is one kingdom
   the king whereof is darkness
thy forehead is a flight of flowers

thy head is a quick forest
   filled with sleeping birds
thy breasts are swarms of white bees
   upon the bough of thy body
thy body to me is April
in whose armpits is the approach of spring

thy thighs are white horses yoked to a chariot
   of kings
they are the striking of a good minstrel
between them is always a pleasant song

my love
thy head is a casket
   of the cool jewel of thy mind
the hair of thy head is one warrior
   innocent of defeat
thy hair upon thy shoulders is an army
   with victory and with trumpets

thy legs are the trees of dreaming
whose fruit is the very eatage of forgetfulness

thy lips are satraps in scarlet
   in whose kiss is the combining of kings
thy wrists
are holy
   which are the keepers of the keys of thy blood
thy feet upon thy ankles are flowers in vases
   of silver

in thy beauty is the dilemma of flutes

    thy eyes are the betrayal
of bells comprehended through incense

|||

listen
beloved
i dreamed
   it appeared that you thought to
   escape me and became a great
   lily atilt on
   insolent
   waters   but i was aware of
   fragrance and i came riding upon
   a horse of porphyry   into the
   waters i rode down the red
   horse shrieking   from splintering
   foam caught you clutched you upon my
   mouth
listen
beloved
   i dreamed   in my dream you had
   desire to thwart me and became
   a little bird and hid
   in a tree of tall marble
   from a great way i distinguished
   singing and i came
   riding upon a scarlet sunset
   trampling the night   easily
   from the shocked impossible
   tower i caught
   you strained you

       broke you upon my blood
listen
       beloved i dreamed
       i thought you would have deceived
       me and became a star in the kingdom
       of heaven
       through day and space i saw you close
       your eyes   and i came riding
       upon a thousand crimson years arched with agony
       i reined them in tottering before
       the throne and as
       they shied at the automaton moon from
       the transplendent hand of sombre god
       i picked you
as an apple is picked by the little peasants for their girls

IV

       unto thee i
       burn incense
       the bowl crackles
       upon the gloom arise purple pencils

       fluent spires of fragrance
       the bowl
       seethes
       a flutter of stars

       a turbulence of forms
       delightful with indefinable flowering,
       the air is
       deep with desirable flowers

       i think
       thou lovest incense

for in the ambiguous faint aspirings
the indolent frail ascensions,

of thy smile rises the immaculate
sorrow
of thy low
hair flutter the level litanies

unto thee i burn
incense,over the dim smoke
straining my lips are vague with
ecstasy my palpitating breasts inhale the

slow
supple
flower
of thy beauty,my heart discovers thee

unto
whom i
burn
olbanum

V

lean candles hunger in
the silence a
brown god
smiles between greentwittering

smokes   from broken eyes
a sound
of strangling breasts and bestial
grovelling

hands rasps the purple
dark-
ness
a

worshipper
prostrate within twitching shadow
lolls

sobbing

with lust

VI

I.

the emperor
sleeps in a palace of porphyry
which was a million years building
he takes the air in a howdah
of jasper beneath saffron
umbrellas
upon an elephant
twelve feet high
behind whose ear
sits always a crowned
king twir-
ling an
ankus of
ebony
the fountains of the emperor's
palace run sunlight and

moonlight and the emperor's
elephant is a thousand years old

the harem of
the emperor
is carpeted with
gold cloth
from the
ceiling(one
diamond timid
with nesting incense)
fifty
marble
pillars
slipped from immeasurable
height,fall,fifty,silent

in the incense is tangled a cool moon

there are thrice-three-hundred
doors carven of chalcedony and
before every door a naked
eunuch watches
on their heads turbans of a hundred
colours
in their hands scimitars like windy torches
each
is
blacker than oblivion

the ladies
of the emperor's
harem are queens
of all the earth and the rings
upon their hands are from mines
a mile deep
but the body of
the queen of queens is

more transparent
than water,she is softer than birds

2.

when the emperor is very
amorous he reclines upon
the couch of couches and
beckons   with
the little
finger of his left
hand
then the
thrice-three-hundredth
door is opened by the tallest
eunuch and the queen
of queens comes
forth
ankles
musical with large pearls
kingdoms in her ears

at the feet of
the emperor a cithern-
player squats with
quiveringgold
body
behind
the emperor ten
elected warriors with
bodies of lazy jade
and twitching
eyelids
finger
their
unquiet
spears

the queen of queens is dancing

her subtle
body weaving
insinuating upon the gold cloth
incessantly creates patterns of sudden
lust
her
stealing body ex-
pending gathering pouring upon itself   stiffenS
to a
white thorn
of desire

the taut neck of the citharede wags
in the dust the ghastly warriors
amber with lust breathe
together   the emperor,exerting
himself among his pillows throws
jewels at the queen of queens and
white money upon her nakedness
he
nods
        and all
depart through the bruised air aflutter with pearls

3.

they are
alone
he beckons,she rises she
stands
a moment
in the passion of the fifty
pillars
listening

while the queens of all the
earth writhe upon deep rugs

AMORES

I

your little voice
             Over the wires came leaping
and i felt suddenly
dizzy
       With the jostling and shouting of merry flowers
wee skipping high-heeled flames
courtesied before my eyes
                or twinkling over to my side
Looked up
with impertinently exquisite faces
floating hands were laid upon me
I was whirled and tossed into delicious dancing
up
Up
with the pale important
               stars and the Humorous
                    moon
dear girl
How i was crazy how i cried when i heard
                 over time
and tide and death
leaping
Sweetly
      your voice

II

      in the rain-
      darkness,   the sunset
      being sheathed i sit and
      think of you

the holy
city which is your face
your little cheeks the streets
of smiles

your eyes half-
thrush
half-angel and your drowsy
lips where float flowers of kiss

and
there is the sweet shy pirouette
your hair
and then

your dancesong
soul.   rarely-beloved
a single star is
uttered,and i

think
       of you

|||

there is a
moon sole
in the blue
night

       amorous of waters
tremulous,
blinded with silence the
undulous heaven yearns where

in tense starlessness
anoint with ardor
the yellow lover

stands in the dumb dark
svelte
and
urgent

        (again
love i slowly
gather
of thy languorous mouth the

thrilling
flower)

IV

consider O
woman this
my body.
for it has

lain
with empty arms
upon the giddy hills
to dream of you,

approve these
firm unsated
eyes
which have beheld

night's speechless carnival
the painting

of the dark
with meteors

streaming from playful
immortal hands
the bursting
of the wafted stars

(in time to come you shall
remember of this night amazing
ecstasies   slowly,
in the glutted

heart fleet
flowerterrible
memories
shall

rise,slowly
return upon the
                    red elected lips

scaleless visions)

V

as is the sea marvelous
from god's
hands which sent her forth
to sleep upon the world

and the earth withers
the moon crumbles
one by one
stars flutter into dust

but the sea
does not change
and she goes forth out of hands and
she returns into hands

and is with sleep....

love,
    the breaking

of your
        soul
          upon
my lips

VI

into the smiting
sky tense
with
blend

ing
the
tree   leaps
          a stiffened exquisite

i
wait the sweet
annihilation of swift
flesh

i make me stern against
your charming strength

O haste
      annihilator
drawing into you my enchanting
leaves

VII

if i believe
in death be sure
of this
it is

because you have loved me,
moon and sunset
stars and flowers
gold crescendo and silver muting

of seatides
i trusted not,
        one night
when in my fingers

drooped your shining body
when my heart
sang between your perfect
breasts

darkness and beauty of stars
was on my mouth petals danced
against my eyes
and down

the singing reaches of
my soul
spoke
the green-

greeting pale-
departing irrevocable
sea
i knew thee death.

                        and when
i have offered up each fragrant
night,when all my days
shall have before a certain

face become
white
perfume
only,

        from the ashes
then
thou wilt rise and thou
wilt come to her and brush

the mischief from her eyes and fold
her
mouth the new
flower with

thy unimaginable
wings,where dwells the breath
of all persisting stars

VIII

the glory is fallen out of
the sky the last immortal
leaf
is

dead and the gold
year
a formal spasm
in the

dust
this is the passing of all shining things
therefore we also
blandly

into receptive
earth,O let
us
descend

take
shimmering wind
these fragile splendors from
us crumple them hide

them in thy breath drive
them in nothingness
for we
would sleep

this is the passing of all shining things
no lingering no backward-
wondering be unto
us O

soul,but straight
glad feet fearruining
and glorygirded
faces

lead us
into the
serious
steep

darkness

IX

i like
to think that on
the flower you gave me when we
loved

    the far-
departed mouth sweetly-saluted
lingers.
      if one marvel

seeing the hunger of my
lips for a dead thing,
i shall instruct
him silently with becoming

steps to seek
your face   and i
entreat,by certain foolish perfect
hours

    dead too,
if that he come receive
him as your lover sumptuously
being

kind
    because i trust him to
your grace,and for
in his own land

he is called death.

X

after five
times the poem
of thy remembrance
surprises with refrain

of unreasoning summer
that by responding
ways cloaked with renewal
my body turns toward

thee
again for the stars have been
finished in the nobler trees and
the language of leaves repeats

eventual perfection
while east deserves of dawn.
i lie at length,breathing
with shut eyes

the sweet earth where thou liest

XI

O Distinct
Lady of my unkempt adoration
if i have made
a fragile certain

song under the window of your soul
it is not like any songs
(the singers the others
they have been faithful

to many things and which
die
i have been sometimes true
to Nothing and which lives

they were fond of the handsome
moon   never spoke ill of the
pretty stars   and to
the serene the complicated

and the obvious
they were faithful
and which i despise,
frankly

admitting i have been true
only to the noise of worms.
in the eligible day
under the unaccountable sun)

Distinct Lady
swiftly take
my fragile certain song
that we may watch together

how behind the doomed
exact smile of life's
placid obscure palpable
carnival where to a normal

melody of probable violins dance
the square virtues and the oblong sins
perfectly
gesticulate the accurate

strenuous lips of incorruptible
Nothing   under the ample
sun,under the insufficient
day under the noise of worms

LA GUERRE

|

Humanity i love you
because you would rather black the boots of
success than enquire whose soul dangles from his
watch-chain which would be embarrassing for both

parties and because you
unflinchingly applaud all
songs containing the words country home and
mother when sung at the old howard

Humanity i love you because
when you're hard up you pawn your
intelligence to buy a drink and when
you're flush pride keeps

you from the pawn shop and
because you are continually committing
nuisances but more
especially in your own house

Humanity i love you because you
are perpetually putting the secret of
life in your pants and forgetting
it's there and sitting down

on it
and because you are
forever making poems in the lap
of death Humanity

i hate you

II

earth like a tipsy
biddy with an old mop punching
underneath
conventions exposes

hidden obscenities
nudging
into neglected sentiments brings
to light dusty

heroisms
and
finally colliding with the most
expensive furniture upsets

a
crucifix which smashes into several
pieces and is hurriedly picked up and
thrown on the ash-heap

where
lies
              what was once the discobolus of
one

Myron

III

the bigness of cannon
is skilful,

but i have seen
death's clever enormous voice

which hides in a fragility
of poppies....

i say that sometimes
on these long talkative animals
are laid fists of huger silence.

I have seen all the silence
filled with vivid noiseless boys

at Roupy
i have seen
between barrages,

the night utter ripe unspeaking girls.

IV

little ladies more
than dead exactly dance
in my head,precisely
dance where danced la guerre.

Mimi à
la voix fragile
qui chatouille Des
Italiens

the putain with the ivory throat
Marie Louise Lallemand
n'est-ce pas que je suis belle
chéri? les anglais m'aiment
tous,les américains
aussi...."bon dos,bon cul de Paris"(Marie

Vierge
Priez
Pour
Nous)

with the
long lips of
Lucienne which dangle
the old men and hot
men se promènent
doucement le soir(ladies

accurately dead les anglais
sont gentils et les américains
aussi,ils payent bien les américains dance

exactly in my brain voulez-
vous coucher avec
moi? Non? pourquoi?)

ladies skilfully
dead precisely dance
where has danced la
guerre j'm'appelle
Manon,cinq rue Henri Monnier
voulez–vous coucher avec moi?
te ferai Mimi
te ferai Minette,
dead exactly dance
si vous voulez
chatouiller
mon lézard ladies suddenly
j'm'en fous des nègres

                    (in the twilight of Paris
Marie Louise with queenly
legs cinq rue Henri

Monnier a little love
begs,Mimi with the body
like une boîte à joujoux,want nice sleep?
toutes les petites femmes exactes
qui dansent toujours in my
head dis–donc,Paris

ta gorge mystérieuse
pourquoi se promène–t–elle,pourquoi
éclate ta voix
fragile couleur de pivoine?)
                              with the

long lips of Lucienne which
dangle the old men and hot men
precisely dance in my head
ladies carefully dead

V

O sweet spontaneous
earth how often have
the
doting

        fingers of
prurient philosophers pinched
and
poked

thee
,has the naughty thumb
of science prodded
thy

              beauty   .how
often have religions taken
thee upon their scraggy knees
squeezing and

buffeting thee that thou mightest conceive
gods
      (but
true

to the incomparable
couch of death thy
rhythmic
lover

        thou answerest

them only with

              spring)

IMPRESSIONS

|

Lady of Silence
from the winsome cage of
thy body
rose
        through the sensible
night
a
quick bird

(tenderly upon
the dark's prodigious face
thy
voice
        scattering perfume-gifted
wings
suddenly escorts
with feet
sun-sheer

the smarting beauty of dawn)

||

the sky a silver
dissonance by the correct
fingers of April
resolved

        into a
clutter of trite jewels

now like a moth with stumbling

wings flutters and flops along the
grass collides with trees and
houses and finally,
butts into the river

III

writhe and
gape of tortured

perspective
rasp and graze of splintered

normality
                crackle and
                        sag
of planes   clamors of
collision
collapse   As

peacefully,
lifted
into the awful beauty
                                of sunset

                        the young city
putting off dimension with a blush
enters
the becoming garden of her agony

IV

the hills
like poets put on
purple thought against
the

magnificent clamor of
                        day

tortured
in gold, which presently

crumpled
collapses
exhaling a red soul into the dark

so
duneyed master
enter
the sweet gates

                        of my heart and

take
the
rose,

which perfect
is
With killing hands

V

stinging
gold swarms
upon the spires
silver

        chants the litanies the
great bells are ringing with rose
the lewd fat bells
                and a tall

wind
is dragging
the
sea

with

dream

-S

VI

the
    sky
            was
can   dy lu
minous
            edible
spry
        pinks shy
lemons
greens   coo l choc
olate
s.

 un   der,
 a   lo
co
mo
       tive   s pout
                   ing
                      vi
                      o
                      lets

VII

i was considering how
within night's loose
sack a star's
nibbling in-

fin
-i-
tes-
i
-mal-
ly devours

darkness the
hungry star
which
will e

-ven
tu-
al
-ly jiggle
the bait of
dawn and be jerked

into

eternity. when over my head a
shooting
star
Bur   s

              (t
                    into a stale shriek
like an alarm-clock)

VIII

between green
                    mountains
sings the flinger
of

fire   beyond red rivers
of fair perpetual
feet the
sinuous

            riot

the
flashing
bacchant.

partedpetaled
mouth,face
delirious.   indivisible
grace

        of dancing

IX

the hours rise up putting off stars and it is
dawn
into the street of the sky light walks scattering poems

on earth a candle is
extinguished   the city
wakes

with a song upon her
mouth having death in her eyes

and it is dawn
the world
goes forth to murder dreams....

i see in the street where strong
men are digging bread
and i see the brutal faces of
people contented hideous hopeless cruel happy

and it is day,

in the mirror
i see a frail
man
dreaming
dreams
dreams in the mirror

and it
is dusk   on earth

a candle is lighted
and it is dark.
the people are in their houses
the frail man is in his bed
the city

sleeps with death upon her mouth having a song in her eyes
the hours descend,
putting on stars....

in the street of the sky night walks scattering poems

X

i will wade out
                        till my thighs are steeped in burning flowers
I will take the sun in my mouth
and leap into the ripe air
                        Alive
                                    with closed eyes
to dash against darkness
                        in the sleeping curves of my body
Shall enter fingers of smooth mastery
with chasteness of sea-girls
                        Will i complete the mystery
                        of my flesh
I will rise
            After a thousand years
lipping
flowers
            And set my teeth in the silver of the moon

PORTRAITS

I

of my
soul a street is:
prettinesses Pic-
abian tricktrickclickflick-er
garnished
of stark Picasso
throttling trees

hither
my soul

repairs herself with
prisms of sharp mind
and Matisse rhythms
to juggle Kandinsky gold-fish

away from the gripping gigantic
muscles of Cézanne's
logic,
      oho.
      a street
there is

where strange birds   purr

          ||

    being
    twelve
    who hast merely
    gonorrhea

          Oldeyed
    child,to
    ambitious weeness
    of boots

    tiny
    add
    death
    what

    shall?

III

as usual i did not find him in cafes,the more dissolute atmosphere
of a street superimposing a numbing imperfectness upon such peregri-
nations as twilight spontaneously by inevitable tiredness of flang-
ing shop-girls impersonally affords furnished a soft first clue to
his innumerable whereabouts   violet logic of annihilation demon-
strating from woolworthian pinnacle a capable millennium of faces
meshing with my curiously instant appreciation exposed his hiber-
native contours,
aimiable immensity impeccably extending the courtesy of five o'clock
became the omen of his presence   it was spring by the way in the
soiled canary-cage of largest existence

(when he would extemporise the innovation of muscularity upon the
most crimson assistance of my comforter a click of deciding glory
inflicted to the negative silence that primeval exposure whose elec-
tric solidity remembers some accurately profuse scratchings in a
recently discovered cave,   the carouse of geometrical putrescence
whereto my invariably commendable room has been forever subject his
Earliest word wheeled out on the sunny dump of oblivion)

a tiny dust finely arising at the integration of my soul i coughed

,naturally

IV

the skinny voice

of the leatherfaced
woman with the crimson
nose and coquettishly-
cocked bonnet

having ceased   the

captain
announces that as three
dimes seven nickels and ten
pennies have been deposited upon

the drum   there is need

of just twenty five cents
dear friends
to make it an even
dollar   whereupon

the Divine Average who was

attracted by the inspired
sister's howling moves
off
will anyone tell him why he should

blow two bits for the coming of Christ Jesus

?
??
???
!

nix,kid

V

Babylon slim
-ness of
evenslicing
eyes are chisels

scarlet Goes
with her
whitehot
face,gashed

by hair's blue cold

jolts of
lovecrazed abrupt

flesh split "Pretty
Baby"
to
numb rhythm before christ

VI

the dress was a suspicious madder,importing the cruelty of roses.
The exciting simplicity of her hipless body,pausing to invent im-
perceptible bulgings of the pretended breasts,forked in surpris-
able unliving eyes chopped by a swollen inanity of picture hat.

the arms hung ugly.,the hands sharp and impertinently dead.

expression began with the early cessation of her skirt.   flesh-
less melody of the,keenly lascivious legs.   painful ankles large
acute brutal feet propped on irrelevantly ferocious heels.

Her gasping slippery body moved with the hideous spontaneity

of a solemn mechanism.   beneath her drab tempo of hasteful futility
lived brilliantly the enormous rhythm of absurdity.

skin like the poisonous fragility of ice newly formed upon an old
pool.   Her nose was small,exact,stupid.   mouth normal,large,uncle·
hair genuinely artificial,unpleasantly tremendous.

under flat lusts of light her nice concupiscence appeared round-
ed.

if she were alive,death was amusing

VII

of evident invisibles
exquisite the hovering

at the dark portals

of hurt girl eyes

sincere with wonder

a poise a wounding
a beautiful suppression

the accurate boy mouth

now droops the faun head

now the intimate flower dreams

of parted lips
dim upon the syrinx

VIII

the
nimble
heat
had

long on a certain
taut precarious
holiday
frighteningly

performed
and
at tremont and bromfield i
paused a moment because

on the frying
curb the
quiet face
lay

which had been dorothy
and once
permitted
me for

twenty
iron
men
her common purple

soul
the absurd eyelids sulked
enormous
sobs puckered the foolish

breasts the
droll
mouth
wilted

and not old,harry,a
woman in the crowd
whinnied and a man squeezing her
waist said

the cop 's rung for the
wagon but as i was
lifting the horror
of her toylike

head and vainly
tried to
catch one funny
hand opening the hard great

eyes to noone in particular she
gasped almost
loudly
i'm

so
drunG

k,dear

IX

ta
ppin
g
toe

hip
popot
amus Back

gen
teel–ly
lugu–
bri ous

LOOPTHELOOP ^{eyes}

as

fathandsbangrag

X

it's just like a coffin's
inside when you die,
pretentious and
shiny and
not too wide
          dear god

there's a portrait
over the door very notable of
the sultan's nose pullable and rosy
flanked by the scrumptious magdalene
of whoisit and madame
something by gainsborough
                                    just the playthings
                                    for dust   n'est-ce pas

   effendi drifts between
   tables like an old leaf
   between toadstools
he is the cheerfulest of men
   his peaked head smoulders
   like a new turd in April
   his legs are brittle and small
   his feet large and fragile
his queer hands twitter before him,like foolish
   butterflies
he is the most courteous of men

should you remark the walls have been repapered

he will nod
            like buddha
            or answer modestly
i am dying

so let us come in together and
drink coffee covered with froth
half-mud
and not too
sweet?

XI

between nose-red gross
walls   sprawling with tipsy
tables the abominable
floor belches smoky

laughter into the filigree
frame of a microscopic
stage whose jouncing curtain.   ,rises
upon one startling doll

undressed in unripe green with
nauseous spiderlegs
and excremental
hair and the eyes of the mother of

god who spits seeds of dead
song about home and love from her
transfigured face a queer
pulp of ecstasy

while in the battered
bodies the odd unlovely
souls struggle   slowly   and   writhe
like caught.brave:flies;

XII

i walked the boulevard

i saw a dirty child
skating on noisy wheels of joy

pathetic dress fluttering

behind her a mothermonster
with red grumbling face

cluttered in pursuit

pleasantly elephantine

while nearby the father

a thick cheerful man

with majestic bulbous lips
and forlorn piggish hands

joked to a girlish whore

with busy rhythmic mouth
and silly purple eyelids

of how she was with child

XIII

5
derbies-with-men-in-them smoke Helmar
cigarettes   2
play backgammon,3 watch

a has gold
teeth b pink

suspenders c
reads Atlantis

x and y play   b
cries "effendi" "Uh" "coffee"
"uh"   enter
paperboy,c

buys Bawstinamereekin,exit
paperboy   a finishes
Helmar   lights
another

          x and y
play,effendi approaches,sets
down coffee   withdraws
a and c discuss news in

turkish x and y play b spits
x and
y
play,b starts armenian record

                              pho
nographisrunn
ingd o   w,   n   phonograph
                              stopS.

b swears in persian at phonograph
x wins   exeunt ax:by;c,
Goo dnightef fendi
....

five men in derbies

XIV

the young
man sitting
in Dick Mid's Place
said to Death

teach me of her
Thy yonder servant who
in Thy very house silently
sits looking beyond the

kissing and the striving of
that old man who at her
redstone mouth renews his
childhood

and He
said
"willingly
for the tale is short

it was
i think yourself delivered into
both my hands herself to
always keep"

always?
the young
man sitting in Dick Mid's
Place

asked
"always"
Death
said

"then as i recollect her
girlhood was by the kindly
lips and body fatherly of a
romantic tired business man

somewhat tweaked and dinted
then
did my servant
become of the company of those

ladies with faces painteaten
and bodies lightly
desperate certainly wherefrom
departed is youth's indispensable

illusion"

XV

one April dusk the
sallow street-lamps were turning
snowy against a west of robin's egg blue when
i entered a mad street whose

mouth dripped with slavver of
spring
chased two flights of squirrel-stairs into
a mid-victorian attic which is known as
Ο ΠΑΡΘΕΝΩΝ
                              and having ordered
yaoorti from
Nicho'
settled my feet on the

ceiling inhaling six divine inches
of Haremina   in
the thick of the snick-
er of cards and smack of back-

gammon boards i was aware of an entirely
dirty circle of habitués their

faces like cigarettebutts, chewed
with disdain,   led by a Jumpy

Tramp who played each
card as if it were a thunderbolt red-
hot   peeling
off huge slabs of a fuzzy

language with the aid of an exclamatory
tooth-pick
And who may that
be i said exhaling into

eternity as Nicho' laid
before me bread
more downy than street-lamps
upon an almostclean

plate
"Achilles"
said
Nicho'

"and did you perhaps wish also shishkabob?"

XVI

between the breasts
of bestial
Marj lie large
men who praise

Marj's cleancornered strokable
body   these men's
fingers toss trunks
shuffle sacks spin kegs they

curl
loving
around
beers

          the world has
these men's hands but their
bodies big and boozing
belong to

Marj
the greenslim purse of whose
face opens
on a fatgold

grin
hooray
hoorah for the large
men who lie

between the breasts
of bestial Marj
for the strong men
who

sleep between the legs of Lil

XVII

but the other
day i was passing a certain
gate,   rain
fell(as it will

in spring)
ropes
of silver gliding from sunny
thunder into freshness

as if god's flowers were
pulling upon bells of
gold   i looked
up

and
thought to myself   Death
and will You with
elaborate fingers possibly touch

the pink hollyhock existence whose
pansy eyes look from morning till
night into the street
unchangingly   the always

old lady always sitting in her
gentle window like
a reminiscence
partaken

softly   at whose gate smile
always the chosen
flowers of reminding

XVIII

inthe,exquisite;

morning   sure   lyHer eye s exactly sit,ata little roundtable
among otherlittle roundtables   Her,eyes   count   slow(ly

obstre peroustimidi ties surElyfl)oat   iNg,the

ofpieces ofof sunligh tof fa l l in gof throughof treesOf.

(Fields Elysian

the like,a)slEEping neck a breathing a   ,lies
(slo wlythe wom an pa)ris her
flesh:wakes
            in little streets

while exactlygir lisHlegs;play;ing;nake;D
and

chairs wait under the trees

Fields slowly Elysian in
a firmcool–Ness   taxis, s.QuirM

and, b etw ee nch air st ott er s thesillyold
WomanSellingBalloonS

In theex qui site

morning,
        her sureLyeye s sit–ex actly her sitsat a surely!little,
roundtable amongother;littleexactly round.   tables,

Her
   .eyes

XIX

the rose
is dying the
lips of an old man murder

the petals
hush
mysteriously
invisible mourners move
with prose faces and sobbing,garments
The symbol of the rose

motionless
with grieving feet and
wings
mounts

against the margins of steep song
a stallion sweetness   ,the

lips of an old man murder

the petals.

XX

spring omnipotent goddess thou dost
inveigle into crossing sidewalks the
unwary june-bug and the frivolous angleworm
thou dost persuade to serenade his
lady the musical tom-cat,thou stuffest
the parks with overgrown pimply
cavaliers and gumchewing giggly

girls and not content
Spring,with this
thou hangest canary-birds in parlor windows

spring slattern of seasons you
have dirty legs and a muddy
petticoat,drowsy is your
mouth your eyes are sticky
with dreams and you have
a sloppy body
from being brought to bed of crocuses
When you sing in your whiskey-voice

                                        the grass
rises on the head of the earth
and all the trees are put on edge

spring,
of the jostle of
thy breasts and the slobber
of your thighs
i am so very
                glad that the soul inside me Hollers
for thou comest and your hands
are the snow
and thy fingers are the rain,
and i hear
the screech of dissonant
flowers,and most of all
i hear your stepping
                        freakish feet
                        feet incorrigible
ragging the world,

XXI

Buffalo Bill 's
defunct
     who used to
     ride a watersmooth-silver
                        stallion
and break onetwothreefourfive pigeonsjustlikethat
                               Jesus

he was a handsome man
                and what i want to know is
how do you like your blueeyed boy
Mister Death

XXII

Cleopatra built
like a smooth arrow or
a fleet pillar is eaten
by yesterday

she was a silver tube of wise
lust whose arms and legs
like white squirming pipes
wiggle upon the perfumed roman

strength who how
furiously plays the hot
sweet horrible stops of
her

body
Cleopatra had a
body
it was

thick slim warm moist
built like an organ
and it
loved

he
was a roman   theirs was a
music sinuous globular
slippery intense witty huge

and its chords
brittle eager eternal luminous
firmly diminishing have swoopingly
fallen svelte sagging gone into the soaring silence

(put
your smallest
ear against yester-
day My Lady   hear

the purple trumpets
blow   horses of gold
delicately crouching beneath silver
youths   the leaneyed

Caesars borne neatly through enormous
twilight surrounded by their triumphs
and
        listen well

how the dainty destroyed
hero clamps the hearty sharp
column
of Egypt

                ,built like a fleet
pillar or a smooth

arrow
Cleopatra is eaten by

yester-
day)
           O i tell you out of
the minute incessant Was irrevocably

emanates a dignity of papyruscoloured
faces   superbly limp
the ostensible centuries
therefore let us be

a little uncouth and amorous in
memory of Cleopatra and of
Antony
and we will

confuse hotly our moreover irrevocable
bodies while the infinite processions
move like moths and like boys and
like incense and like sunlight

and like ships and like young girls and like
butterflies and like money
and like laughter
and like elephants

through our
single
brain   in memory of Cleopatra   while
easily

tremendously
floats
in the bright shouting street of time
her nakedness with its blue hair

(all is eaten by yester-
day
between the nibbling timid teethful hours
wilts the stern texture of Now

the arrow and the
pillar pursue curiously
a crumbling flight into the absolute stars
the gods are swallowed

even
Nile
the
kind black great god)

Cleopatra you
are eaten
by yester-
day

(and O My Lady Lady Of
Ladies you
who move beautifully in the winds
of my lust like a high troubling

ship upon the fragrant
unspeaking ignorant darkness of New
Lady whose kiss is
a procession of deep beasts

coming with keen ridiculous
silks coming with sharp languid perfumes
coming with the little profound gems and
the large laughing stones

a sinuous problem of colour
floating against

the clever deadly
heaven   i salute

you
whose body is
Egypt
whose hair is Nile)

put your ear
to the ground
there is a music
Lady

            the noiseless truth of swirling
worms
is
tomorrow

XXIII

Picasso
you give us Things
which
bulge:grunting lungs pumped full of sharp thick mind

you make us shrill
presents always
shut in the sumptuous screech of
simplicity

(out of the
black unbunged
Something gushes vaguely a squeak of planes
or

between squeals of
Nothing grabbed with circular shrieking tightness
solid screams whisper.)
Lumberman of The Distinct

your brain's
axe only chops hugest inherent
Trees of Ego,from
whose living and biggest

bodies lopped
of every
prettiness

you hew form truly

XXIV

conversation with my friend is particularly

to enjoy the composed sudden body atop which always quiv-
ers the electric Distinct face haughtily vital clinched
in a swoon of synopsis

despite a sadistic modesty his mind is seen frequently
fingering the exact beads of a faultless languor when
invisibly consult with some delicious image the a little
strolling lips and eyes inwardly crisping

for my friend,feeling is the sacred and agonizing prox-
imity to its desire of a doomed impetuous acute sentience
whose whitehot lips however suddenly approached may never
quite taste the wine which their nearness evaporates

to think is the slippery contours of a vase inexpressibly
fragile it is for the brain irrevocably frigid to touch a
merest shape which however slenderly by it caressed will
explode and spill the immediate imperceptible content

my friend's being,out of the spontaneous clumsy trivial
acrobatic edgeless gesture of existence,continually whit-
tles keen careful futile flowers

(isolating with perpetually meticulous concupiscence the
bright large undeniable disease of Life,himself occasion-
ally contrives an unreal precise intrinsic fragment of
actuality),

an orchid whose velocity is sculptural

XXV

my mind is
a big hunk of irrevocable nothing which touch and taste and smell
and hearing and sight keep hitting and chipping with sharp fatal
tools
in an agony of sensual chisels i perform squirms of chrome and ex-
ecute strides of cobalt
nevertheless i
feel that i cleverly am being altered that i slightly am becoming
something a little different,in fact
myself
Hereupon helpless i utter lilac shreiks and scarlet bellowings.

XXVI

the waddling
madam star
taps
taps.   "ready girls".   the

unspontaneous streets
make bright their eyes
a
blind irisher fiddles a

scotch jig in a stinking
joyman bar
a cockney is
buying whiskies for a turk

a waiter intones:bloo–moo–n
sirkusricky
platzburg
hoppytoad   yesmam.   the

furious taximan
p(ee)ps
on his whistle somebody
says here's luck

somebody else says down the hatch
the nigger smiles
the jew stands
beside his teddy-bears

the sailor shuffles the
night with fucking eyes
the great black preacher gargles jesus
the aesthete indulges

his soul for certain things which died
it is eighteen hundred
years....
exactly

under the window
under the window
under the window walk

the unburied feet of
the little ladies more than dead

XXVII

her
flesh
Came
at

meassandca V
            ingint
                        oA
chute
      i had cement for her,
      merrily
we became each
other humped to tumbling

garble   when
a
minute
pulled the sluice

                  emerging.

concrete

XXVIII

raise the shade
will youse dearie?
rain
wouldn't that

get yer goat but
we don't care do
we dearie we should
worry about the rain

huh
dearie?
yknow
i'm

sorry for awl the
poor girls that
gets up god
knows when every

day of their
lives
aint you,
                oo–oo.   dearie

not so
hard dear

you're killing me

XXIX

somebody knew Lincoln somebody Xerxes

this man:a narrow thudding timeshaped face
plus innocuous winking hands,carefully
inhabits number 1 on something street

Spring comes
                    the lean and definite houses

are troubled.   A sharp blue day
fills with peacefully leaping air
the minute mind of the world.
The lean and

definite houses are
troubled.in the sunset their chimneys converse
angrily,their
roofs are nervous with the soft furious
light,and while fire-escapes and
roofs and chimneys and while roofs and fire-escapes and
chimneys and while chimneys and fire-escapes
and roofs are talking rapidly all together there happens
Something,and They

cease(and
one by one are turned suddenly and softly
into irresponsible toys.)
                    when this man with

the brittle legs winces
swiftly out of number 1 someThing
street and trickles carefully into the park
sits

Down.   pigeons circle
around and around and around the

irresponsible toys
circle wildly in the slow-ly-in creasing fragility
—.Dogs
bark
children
play
-ing
    Are

in the beautiful nonsense of twilight

and somebody Napoleon

POST IMPRESSIONS

|

windows go orange in the slowly.
town,   night
featherly swifts
the
    Dark on us
all;
    stories told returned

    gather

    the

Again:who
danc   ing
goes utter   ly

churning
witty,twitters

upon Our

(ta-te-ta
in a parenthesis!said the moon

)

||

beyond the brittle towns asleep
i look where stealing needles of foam
in the last light

thread the creeping shores

as out of dumb strong hands infinite

the erect deep upon me
in the last light
pours its eyeless miles

the chattering sunset ludicrously
dies,i hear only tidewings

in the last light
twitching at the world

III

the moon is hiding in
her hair.
The
lily
of heaven
full of all dreams,
draws down.

cover her briefness in singing
close her with intricate faint birds
by daisies and twilights
Deepen her,

Recite
upon her
flesh
the rain's

pearls singly-whispering.

IV

riverly is a flower
gone softly by tomb
rosily gods whiten
befall saith rain

anguish
and dream-send is
hushed
in

moan-loll where
night   gathers
morte carved smiles

cloud–gloss is at moon–cease
soon
verbal mist-flowers close
ghosts on prowl gorge

sly slim gods stare

V

any man is wonderful
and a formula
a bit of tobacco and gladness
plus little derricks of gesture

any skyscraper
bulges in the looseness of morning
but in twilight becomes
unutterably crisp

a thing,
which tightens
caught
in the hoisting light

any woman is smooth and ridiculous
a polite uproar of knuckling silent planes
a nudging bulb silkenly brutal
a devout flexion

VI

into the strenuous briefness
Life:
handorgans and April
darkness,friends

i charge laughing.
Into the hair-thin tints
of yellow dawn,
into the women-coloured twilight

i smilingly
glide.   I
into the big vermilion departure
swim,sayingly;

(Do you think?)the
i do,world
is probably made
of roses & hello:

(of solongs and,ashes)

VII

at the head of this street a gasping organ is waving moth-eaten
tunes.   a fattish hand turns the crank;the box spouts fairies,out
of it sour gnomes tumble clumsily,the little box is spilling ran-
cid elves upon neat sunlight into the flowerstricken air which is
filthy with agile swarming sonal creatures

—Children,stand with circular frightened faces glaring at the
shabby tiny smiling,man in whose hand the crank goes desperately,
round and round pointing to the queer monkey

(if you toss him a coin he will pick it cleverly from,the air and
stuff it seriously in,his minute pocket)Sometimes he does not
catch a piece of money and then his master will yell at him over
the music and jerk the little string and the monkey will sit,up,
and look at,you with his solemn blinky eyeswhichneversmile and
after he has caught a,penny or three,pennies he will be thrown a
peanut(which he will open skilfully with his,mouth carefully
holding,it,in his little toylike hand)and then he will stiff-ly
throw the shell away with a small bored gesture that makes the
children laugh.

But i don't,   the crank goes round desperate elves and hopeless
gnomes and frantic fairies gush clumsily from the battered box
fattish and mysterious the flowerstricken sunlight is thickening
dizzily is reeling gently the street and the children and the mon-
keyandtheorgan and the man are dancing slowly are tottering up
and down in a trembly mist of atrocious melody....tiniest dead
tunes crawl upon my face my hair is lousy with mutilated singing
microscopic things in my ears scramble faintly tickling putres-
cent atomies,
                    and
                              i feel the jerk of the little string!the tiny
smiling shabby man is yelling over the music i understand him i
shove my round red hat back on my head i sit up and blink at you
with my solemn eyeswhichneversmile

yes,By god.
for i am they are pointing at the queer monkey with a little
oldish doll-like face and hairy arms like an ogre and rubbercolour-
ed hands and feet filled with quick fingers and a remarkable tail
which is allbyitself alive.(and he has a little red coat with i
have a real pocket in it and the round funny hat with a big feather
is tied under myhis chin.)   that climbs and cries and runs and
floats like a toy on the end of a string

VIII

i was sitting in mcsorley's.   outside it was New York and beauti-
fully snowing.

Inside snug and evil.   the slobbering walls filthily push witless
creases of screaming warmth chuck pillows are noise funnily swallows
swallowing revolvingly pompous a the swallowed mottle with smooth or
a but of rapidly goes gobs the and of flecks of and a chatter sobbings
intersect with which distinct disks of graceful oath,upsoarings the
break on   ceiling-flatness

the Bar.tinking luscious jigs dint of ripe silver with warmlyish
wetflat splurging smells waltz the glush of squirting taps plus slush
of foam knocked off and a faint piddle-of-drops she says I ploc spittle
what the lands thaz me kid in no sir hopping sawdust you kiddo he's a
palping wreaths of badly Yep cigars who jim him why gluey grins topple
together eyes pout gestures stickily point made glints squinting who's
a wink bum-nothing and money fuzzily mouths take big wobbly foot-steps
every goggle cent of it get out ears dribbles soft right old feller
belch the chap hic summore eh chuckles skulch....

and i was sitting in the din thinking drinking the ale,which never
lets you grow old blinking at the low ceiling my being pleasantly was
punctuated by the always retchings of a worthless lamp.

when With a minute terrif   iceffort one dirty squeal of soiling light
yanKing from bushy obscurity a bald greenish foetal head established
It suddenly upon the huge neck around whose unwashed sonorous muscle
the filth of a collar hung gently.

(spattered)by this instant of semiluminous nausea A vast wordless
nondescript genie of trunk trickled firmly in to one exactly-mutilated
ghost of a chair,

a;domeshaped interval of complete plasticity,shoulders,sprouted the
extraordinary arms through an angle of ridiculous velocity commenting
upon an unclean table,and,whose distended immense Both paws slowly
loved a dinted mug

gone Darkness   it was so near to me,i ask of shadow won't you have a
drink?

(the eternal perpetual question)

Inside snugandevil.   i was sitting in mcsorley's   It,did not answer.

outside.(it was New York and beautifully,snowing....

IX

at the ferocious phenomenon of 5 o'clock i find myself gently decompos-
ing in the mouth of New York.   Between its supple financial teeth delir-
iously sprouting from complacent gums,a morsel prettily wanders buoy-
ed on the murderous saliva of industry.   the morsel is i.

Vast cheeks enclose me.

a gigantic uvula with imperceptible gesticulations threatens the tubu-
lar downward blackness occasionally from which detaching itself bumps
clumsily into the throat A meticulous vulgarity:

a sodden fastidious normal explosion;a square murmur,a winsome flatu-
lence—

In the soft midst of the tongue sits the Woolworth building a serene
pastile-shaped insipid kinesis or frail swooping lozenge.   a ruglike
sentience whose papillae expertly drink the docile perpendicular taste
of this squirming cube of undiminished silence,supports while devour-
ing the firm tumult of exquisitely insecure sharp algebraic music.
For the first time in sorting from this vast nonchalant inward walk of
volume the flat minute gallop of careful hugeness i am conjugated by
the sensual mysticism of entire vertical being ,i am skilfully con-
strued by a delicately experimenting colossus whose irrefutable spiral

antics involve me with the soothings of plastic hypnotism   .i am ac-
curately parsed by this gorgeous rush of upward lips....

cleverly

perching on the sudden extremity of one immense tooth myself surveys
safely the complete important profane frantic inconsequential gastro-
nomic mystery of mysteries
                                        ,life

Far below myself the lunging leer of horizontal large distinct ecstasy
wags and.rages   Laughters jostle grins nudge smiles push—.   deep into
the edgeless gloaming gladness hammers incessant putrid spikes of mad-
ness (at

Myself's height these various innocent ferocities are superseded by
the sole prostituted ferocity of silence,it is) still 5 o'clock

I stare only always into the tremendous canyon the

,tremendous canyon always only exhales a climbing dark exact walloping
human noise of digestible millions whose rich slovenly obscene proces-
sion always floats through the thin amorous enormous only lips of the
evening

            And it is 5 o'clock

            in the oblong air,from which a singular ribbon of common sunset
is hanging,

snow speaks slowly

SNO

a white idea(Listen

drenches:earth's ugly)mind.
,Rinsing with exact death

the annual brain
                clotted with loosely voices
look
look. Skilfully

.fingered by(a parenthesis
the)pond on whoseswooning edge

black trees think

(hear little knives of flower
stropping sof a.   Thick silence)

blacktreesthink

tiny,angels sharpen:themselves

(on
    air)
don't speak
          A white idea,

drenching.   earth's brain detaches
clottingsand from a a nnual(ugliness

of)rinsed mind slowly:

from!the:A wending putrescence.   a.of,loosely

;voices

XI

i am going to utter a tree,Nobody
shall stop me

but first
earth   ,the reckless oral darkness
raging with thin impulse

i will have

a
    dream
    i
    think it shall be roses and
spring will bring her
worms rushing through loam.

(afterward i'll
climb
by tall careful muscles

into nervous and accurate silence....But   first

you)

press easily
at first,it will be leaves
and a little harder
for roses
only a little harder

last   we
on the groaning flame of neat huge
trudging kiss moistly climbing hideously with
large
minute
hips,O

      .press

worms rushing slowly through loam

CHIMNEYS

SONNETS—REALITIES

I

the Cambridge ladies who live in furnished souls
are unbeautiful and have comfortable minds
(also,with the church's protestant blessings
daughters,unscented shapeless spirited)
they believe in Christ and Longfellow,both dead,
are invariably interested in so many things—
at the present writing one still finds
delighted fingers knitting for the is it Poles?
perhaps.   While permanent faces coyly bandy
scandal of Mrs. N and Professor D
....the Cambridge ladies do not care,above
Cambridge if sometimes in its box of
sky lavender and cornerless,the
moon rattles like a fragment of angry candy

II

when i am in Boston,i do not speak.
and i sit in the click of ivory balls....

noting flies,which jerk upon the weak
colour of table-cloths,the electric When
In Doubt Buy Of(but a roof hugs
whom)
        as the august evening mauls
Kneeland,and a waiter cleverly lugs
indigestible honeycake to men

....one perfectly smooth coffee
tasting of hellas,i drink,or sometimes two
remarking cries of paklavah meeah.
(Very occasionally three.)
and i gaze on the cindercoloured little ΜΕΓΑ
ΕΛΛΗΝΙΚΟΝ ΞΕΝΟΔΟΧΕΙΟΝ ΥΠΝΟΥ

III

goodby Betty,don't remember me
pencil your eyes dear and have a good time
with the tall tight boys at Tabari'
s,keep your teeth snowy,stick to beer and lime,
wear dark,and where your meeting breasts are round
have roses darling,it's all i ask of you—
but that when light fails and this sweet profound
Paris moves with lovers,two and two
bound for themselves,when passionately dusk
brings softly down the perfume of the world
(and just as smaller stars begin to husk
heaven)you,you exactly paled and curled

with mystic lips take twilight where i know:
proving to Death that Love is so and so.

IV

ladies and gentlemen this little girl
with the good teeth and small important breasts
(is it the Frolic or the Century whirl?

one's memory indignantly protests)
this little dancer with the tightened eyes
crisp ogling shoulders and the ripe quite too
large lips always clenched faintly,wishes you
with all her fragile might to not surmise
she dreamed one afternoon

                              ....or maybe read?

of a time when the beautiful most of her
(this here and This,do you get me?)
will maybe dance and maybe sing and be
absitively posolutely dead,
like Coney Island in winter

V

by god i want above fourteenth

fifth's deep purring biceps,the mystic screech
of Broadway,the trivial stink of rich

frail firm asinine life
                        (i pant

for what's below.   the singer.   Wall.   i want
the perpendicular lips the insane teeth
the vertical grin

                    give me the Square in spring,
 the little barbarous Greenwich perfumed fake

And most,the futile fooling labyrinth
where noisy colours stroll....and the Baboon

sniggering insipidities while. i sit,sipping
singular anisettes as.   One opaque
big girl jiggles thickly hips to the kanoon

but Hassan chuckles seeing the Greeks breathe)

VI

when you rang at Dick Mid's Place
the madam was a bulb stuck in the door.
a fang of wincing gas showed how
hair,in two fists of shrill colour,
clutched the dull volume of her tumbling face
scribbled with a big grin. her sow-
eyes clicking mischief from thick lids.
the chunklike nose on which always the four
tablets of perspiration erectly sitting.
—If they knew you at Dick Mid's
the three trickling chins began to traipse
into the cheeks "eet smeestaire steevensun
kum een,dare ease Bet,an Leelee,an dee beeg wun"
her handless wrists did gooey severe shapes.

VII

a fragrant sag of fruit distinctly grouped.

I have not eaten peppers for a week.

On this street the houses immensely speak
(it is nine minutes past six)

the well-fed L's immaculate roar looped
straightens,into neatest distance....

A new curve of children gladly cricks
where a hurdy-gurdy accurately pants.

and pompous ancient jews obscurely twitch
through the bumping teem of Grand. a nudging froth
of faces clogs Second as Mrs. Somethingwich

(with flesh like an old toy balloon)

heavily swims to Strunsky's,

                    Monia's mouth
eats tangerines looking at the moon—

VIII

   irreproachable ladies firmly lewd
on dangerous slabs of tilting din whose
mouths distinctly walk
                  your smiles accuse

the dusk with an untimid svelte subdued
magic
      while in your eyes there lives
a green egyptian noise. ladies with whom time

feeds especially his immense lips

On whose deep nakedness death most believes,
perpetual girls marching to love

whose bodies kiss me with the square crime
of life....Cecile,the oval shove
of hiding pleasure.   Alice,stinging quips
of flesh.   Loretta, cut the comedy
kid....

Fran Mag Glad Dorothy

nearer:breath of my breath:take not thy tingling
limbs from me:make my pain their crazy meal
letting thy tigers of smooth sweetness steal
slowly in dumb blossoms of new mingling:
deeper:blood of my blood:with upwardcringing
swiftness plunge these leopards of white dream
in the glad flesh of my fear:more neatly ream
this pith of darkness:carve an evilfringing
flower of madness on gritted lips
and on sprawled eyes squirming with light insane
chisel the killing flame that dizzily grips.

Querying greys between mouthed houses curl

thirstily.   Dead stars stink.   dawn.   Inane,

the poetic carcass of a girl

X

when thou hast taken thy last applause,and when
the final curtain strikes the world away,
leaving to shadowy silence and dismay

that stage which shall not know thy smile again,
lingering a little while i see thee then
ponder the tinsel part they let thee play;
i see the large lips vivid,the face grey,
and silent smileless eyes of Magdalen.
The lights have laughed their last;without,the street
darkling awaiteth her whose feet have trod
the silly souls of men to golden dust:
she pauses on the lintel of defeat,
her heart breaks in a smile—and she is Lust....

mine also,little painted poem of god

XI

god pity me whom(god distinctly has)
the weightless svelte drifting sexual feather
of your shall i say body?follows
truly through a dribbling moan of jazz

whose arched occasional steep youth swallows
curvingly the keenness of my hips;
or,your first twitch of crisp boy flesh dips
my height in a firm fragile stinging weather,

(breathless with sharp necessary lips)kid

female cracksman of the nifty,ruffian-rogue,
laughing body with wise breasts half-grown,
lisping flesh quick to thread the fattish drone
of I Want a Doll,
                        wispish-agile feet with slid
steps parting the tousle of saxophonic brogue.

XII

"kitty". sixteen,5′1″,white,prostitute.

ducking always the touch of must and shall,
whose slippery body is Death's littlest pal,

skilled in quick softness.   Unspontaneous.   cute.

the signal perfume of whose unrepute
focusses in the sweet slow animal
bottomless eyes importantly banal,

Kitty. a whore. Sixteen
                                    you corking brute
amused from time to time by clever drolls
fearsomely who do keep their sunday flower.
The babybreasted broad "kitty" twice eight

—beer nothing,the lady'll have a whiskey-sour—

whose least amazing smile is the most great
common divisor of unequal souls.

XIII

it started when Bill's chip let on to
the bulls he'd bumped a bloke back in fifteen.
Then she came toward him on her knees across the locked
room.   he knocked her cold and beat it for Chicago.

Eddie was waiting for him,and they cleaned up a few
times—before she got the info
from a broad that knew Eddie in Topeka,went clean
daffy,and which was very silly hocked

the diamond he gave her.   Bill was put wise
that she was coming with his kid inside her.
He laughed.   She came.   he gave her a shove
and asked Eddie did he care to ride her?
....she exactly lay,looking hunks of love

in The Chair he kept talking about eyes

XIV

she sits dropping on a caret of clenched arms
a delicately elephantine face
(It is necessary to find Hassan's Place
by tiny streets shrugging with colour)
the mouth who sits between her cheeks
utters a thud of scarlet. always.   More
interesting,as i think,her charms
en repos....a fattish leg leaks
obscenely from the dress.   one nipple tries.
playfully to peek into the belly
whose deep squirm nibbles. another couches,
weary,upon a flabby mattress of jelly....
than when to the kanoon she totters,slouches,
with giggling hips and frozen eyes

XV

unnoticed woman from whose kind large flesh

i turn to the cruel–littleness of cold
(when battling street-lamps fail upon the gold
dawn,where teeth of slowturning streets mesh

in a frieze of smoking Face Bluish–old

and choked pat of going soles on flat
pavements with icy cries of this and that
stumbling in gloom,bad laughters,smiles unbold)

also,tomorrow the daily papers will feature
Peace and Good Will,and Mary with one lung
extended to the pumping Child,and " 'Twas

the night before Christmas when all through the house not a creature
was stirring,not even a mouse.   The stockings were hung
by the chimney with care in hopes that Saint Nicholas"

XVI

twentyseven bums give a prostitute the once
—over. fiftythree(and one would see if it could)

eyes say the breasts look very good:
firmlysquirmy with a slight jounce,

thirteen pants have a hunch

. admit in threedimensional distress
these hips were made for Horizontal Business
(set on big legs nice to pinch

assiduously which justgraze
each other).   As the lady lazily struts

(her
thickish flesh superior to the genuine daze
of unmarketable excitation,

whose careless movements carefully scatter

pink propaganda of annihilation

XVII

of this wilting wall the colour drub
souring sunbeams,of a foetal fragrance
to rickety unclosed blinds inslants
peregrinate,a cigar-stub
disintegrates,above,underdrawers club
the faintly sweating air with pinkness,
one pale dog behind a slopcaked shrub
painstakingly utters a slippery mess,
a star sleepily,feebly,scratches the sore
of morning.   But i am interested more
intricately in the delicate scorn
with which in a putrid window every day
almost leans a lady whose still-born
smile involves the comedy of decay,

XVIII

whereas by dark really released,the modern
flame of her indomitable body
uses a careful fierceness.   Her lips study
my head gripping for a decision:burn
the terrific fingers which grapple and joke
on my passionate anatomy
oh yes!   Large legs pinch,toes choke—
hair-thin strands of magic agony
....by day this lady in her limousine

oozes in fashionable traffic,just
a halfsmile (for society's sweet sake)
in the not too frail lips almost discussed;
between her and ourselves a nearly-opaque
perfume disinterestedly obscene.

XIX

my girl's tall with hard long eyes
as she stands,with her long hard hands keeping
silence on her dress,good for sleeping
is her long hard body filled with surprise
like a white shocking wire,when she smiles
a hard long smile it sometimes makes
gaily go clean through me tickling aches,
and the weak noise of her eyes easily files
my impatience to an edge—my girl's tall
and taut,with thin legs just like a vine
that's spent all of its life on a garden-wall,
and is going to die.   When we grimly go to bed
with these legs she begins to heave and twine
about me,and to kiss my face and head.

XX

Dick Mid's large bluish face without eyebrows

sits in the kitchen nights and chews a two-bit
cigar
       waiting for the bulls to pull his joint.
Jimmie was a dude.   Dark hair and nice hands.

with a little eye that rolled and made its point

Jimmie's sister worked for Dick.   And had some rows
over percent.   The gang got shot up twice,it
operated in the hundred ands

All the chips would kid Jimmie to give them a kiss
but Jimmie lived regular. stewed three times a week.

and slept twice a week with a big toothless girl
in Yonkers.
                          Dick Mid's green large three teeth leak

smoke:remembering,two pink big lips curl....

how Jimmie was framed and got his

XXI

life boosts herself rapidly at me

through sagging debris of exploded day
the hulking perpendicular mammal
                                                                a
grim epitome of chuckling flesh.
Weak thirsty fists of idiot futures bash

the bragging breasts,
                                        puppy-faces to mouth
her ugly nipples squirming in pretty wrath,
gums skidding on slippery udders

                                                  she
lifts an impertinent puerperal face
and with astute fatuous swallowed eyes
smiles,
              one grin very distinctly wobbles
from the thinning lips me hugely which embrace.
as in the hairy notching of clenched thighs

a friendless dingy female frenzy bubbles

SONNETS—UNREALITIES

I

and what were roses.   Perfume?for i do
forget....or mere Music mounting unsurely

twilight
          but here were something more maturely
childish,more beautiful almost than you.

Yet if not flower,tell me softly who

be these haunters of dreams always demurely
halfsmiling from cool faces,moving purely
with muted step,yet somewhat proudly too—

are they not ladies,ladies of my dream
justly touching roses their fingers whitely
live by?
          or better,
                              queens,queens laughing lightly
crowned with far colours,

                                        thinking very much
of nothing and whom dawn loves most to touch

wishing by willows,bending upon streams?

II

when unto nights of autumn do complain
earth's ghastlier trees by whom Time measured is
when frost to dance maketh the sagest pane
of littler huts with peerless fantasies
or the unlovely longness of the year

droops with things dead athwart the narrowing hours
and hope(by cold espoused unto fear)
in dreadful corners hideously cowers—

i do excuse me,love,to Death and Time

storms and rough cold,wind's menace and leaf's grieving:
from the impressed fingers of sublime
Memory,of that loveliness receiving
the image my proud heart cherished as fair.

(The child-head poised with the serious hair)

III

a connotation of infinity
sharpens the temporal splendor of this night

when souls which have forgot frivolity
in lowliness,noting the fatal flight
of worlds whereto this earth's a hurled dream

down eager avenues of lifelessness

consider for how much themselves shall gleam,
in the poised radiance of perpetualness.
When what's in velvet beyond doomed thought

is like a woman amorous to be known;
and man,whose here is always worse than naught,
feels the tremendous yonder for his own—

on such a night the sea through her blind miles

of crumbling silence seriously smiles

IV

Thou in whose swordgreat story shine the deeds
of history her heroes,sounds the tread
of those vast armies of the marching dead,
with standards and the neighing of great steeds
moving to war across the smiling meads;
thou by whose page we break the precious bread
of dear communion with the past,and wed
to valor,battle with heroic breeds;

thou,Froissart,for that thou didst love the pen
while others wrote in steel,accept all praise
of after ages,and of hungering days
for whom the old glories move,the old trumpets cry;
who gavest as one of those immortal men
his life that his fair city might not die.

V

when my sensational moments are no more
unjoyously bullied of vilest mind

and sweet uncaring earth by thoughtful war
heaped wholly with high wilt of human rind—
when over hate has triumphed darkly love

and the small spiritual cry of spring
utters a striving flower,
                              just where strove
the droll god-beasts

                         do thou distinctly bring
thy footstep,and the rushing of thy deep

hair and the smiting smile didst love to use
in other days (drawing my Mes from sleep
whose stranger dreams thy strangeness must abuse....)

Time being not for us,purple roses were
sweeter to thee
                            perchance to me deeper.

VI

god gloats upon Her stunning flesh.   Upon
the reachings of Her green body among
unseen things,things obscene (Whose fingers young

the caving ages curiously con)

—but the lunge of Her hunger softly flung
over the gasping shores
                            leaves his smile wan,
and his blood stopped hears in the frail anon

the shovings and the lovings of Her tongue.

god Is The Sea.   All terrors of his being
quake before this its hideous Work most old
Whose battening gesture prophecies a freeing

of ghostly chaos
                        in this dangerous night
through moaned space god worships God—

                                            (behold!
where chaste stars writhe captured in brightening fright)

VII

O Thou to whom the musical white spring

offers her lily inextinguishable,
taught by thy tremulous grace bravely to fling

Implacable death's mysteriously sable
robe from her redolent shoulders,
                              Thou from whose
feet reincarnate song suddenly leaping
flameflung,mounts,inimitably to lose
herself where the wet stars softly are keeping

their exquisite dreams—O Love! upon thy dim
shrine of intangible commemoration,
(from whose faint close as some grave languorous hymn

pledged to illimitable dissipation
unhurried clouds of incense fleetly roll)

i spill my bright incalculable soul.

VIII

when the proficient poison of sure sleep
bereaves us of our slow tranquillities

and He without Whose favour nothing is
(being of men called Love) upward doth leap
from the mute hugeness of depriving deep,

with thunder of those hungering wings of His,

into the lucent and large signories
—i shall not smile beloved;i shall not weep:

when from the less-than-whiteness of thy face
(whose eyes inherit vacancy) will time
extract his inconsiderable doom,
when these thy lips beautifully embrace
nothing
        and when thy bashful hands assume

silence beyond the mystery of rhyme

IX

this is the garden:colours come and go,
frail azures fluttering from night's outer wing
strong silent greens serenely lingering,
absolute lights like baths of golden snow.
This is the garden:pursed lips do blow
upon cool flutes within wide glooms,and sing
(of harps celestial to the quivering string)
invisible faces hauntingly and slow.

This is the garden.   Time shall surely reap
and on Death's blade lie many a flower curled,
in other lands where other songs be sung;
yet stand They here enraptured,as among
the slow deep trees perpetual of sleep
some silver-fingered fountain steals the world.

X

it is at moments after i have dreamed
of the rare entertainment of your eyes,
when(being fool to fancy)i have deemed

with your peculiar mouth my heart made wise;
at moments when the glassy darkness holds

the genuine apparition of your smile
(it was through tears always)and silence moulds
such strangeness as was mine a little while;

moments when my once more illustrious arms
are filled with fascination,when my breast
wears the intolerant brightness of your charms:

one pierced moment whiter than the rest

—turning from the tremendous lie of sleep
i watch the roses of the day grow deep.

XI

it may not always be so;and i say
that if your lips,which i have loved,should touch
another's,and your dear strong fingers clutch
his heart,as mine in time not far away;
if on another's face your sweet hair lay
in such a silence as i know,or such
great writhing words as,uttering overmuch,
stand helplessly before the spirit at bay;

if this should be,i say if this should be—
you of my heart,send me a little word;

that i may go unto him,and take his hands,
saying,Accept all happiness from me.
Then shall i turn my face,and hear one bird
sing terribly afar in the lost lands.

XII

I have seen her a stealthily frail
flower walking with its fellows in the death
of light,against whose enormous curve of flesh
exactly cubes of tiny fragrance try;
i have watched certain petals rapidly wish
in the corners of her youth;whom,fiercely shy
and gently brutal,the prettiest wrath
of blossoms dishevelling made a pale
fracas upon the accurate moon....
Across the important gardens her body
will come toward me with its hurting sexual smell
of lilies....beyond night's silken immense swoon
the moon is like a floating silver hell
a song of adolescent ivory.

XIII

if learned darkness from our searched world

should wrest the rare unwisdom of thy eyes,
and if thy hands flowers of silence curled

upon a wish,to rapture should surprise
my soul slowly which on thy beauty dreams
(proud through the cold perfect night whisperless

to mark,how that asleep whitely she seems

whose lips the whole of life almost do guess)

if god should send the morning;and before
my doubting window leaves softly to stir,
of thoughtful trees whom night hath pondered o'er
—and frailties of dimension to occur

about us
        and birds known,scarcely to sing

(heart,could we bear the marvel of this thing?)

XIV

who's most afraid of death?thou
                      art of him
utterly afraid,i love of thee
(beloved)this

         and truly i would be
near when his scythe takes crisply the whim
of thy smoothness. and mark the fainting
murdered petals.   with the caving stem.

But of all most would i be one of them

round the hurt heart which do so fraily cling....)
i who am but imperfect in my fear

Or with thy mind against my mind,to hear
nearing our hearts' irrevocable play—
through the mysterious high futile day

an enormous stride
                    (and drawing thy mouth toward

my mouth,steer our lost bodies carefully downward)

XV

   come nothing to my comparable soul
   which with existence has conversed in vain,
   O scrupulously take thy trivial toll,
   for whose cool feet this frantic heart is fain;
   try me with thy perfumes which have seduced
   the mightier nostrils of the fervent dead,
   feed with felicities me wormperused
   by whom the hungering mouth of time is fed:
   and if i like not what thou givest me
   to him let me complain,whose seat is where
   revolving planets struggle to be free
   with the astounding everlasting air—
   but if i like,i'll take between thy hands
   what no man feels,no woman understands.

XVI

   when citied day with the sonorous homes
   of light swiftly sink in the sorrowful hour,
   thy counted petals O tremendous flower
   on whose huge heart prospecting darkness roams

   torture my spirit with the exquisite froms
   and whithers of existence,
                              as by shores
   soundless,the unspeaking watcher who adores

perceived sails whose mighty brightness dumbs

the utterance of his soul—so even i
wholly chained to a grave astonishment
feel in my being the delirious smart

of thrilled ecstasy,where sea and sky
marry—

        to know the white ship of thy heart

on frailer ports of costlier commerce bent

XVII

will suddenly trees leap from winter and will

the stabbing music of your white youth
wounded by my arms' bothness
(say a twilight lifting the fragile skill
of new leaves' voices,and sharp lips of spring
simply joining with the wonderless
city's sublime cheap distinct mouth)

do the exact human comely thing?

(or will the fleshless moments go and go

across this dirtied pane where softly preys
the grey and perpendicular Always—
or possibly there drift a pulseless blur
of paleness;
             'the unswift mouths of snow
insignificantly whisper....

XVIII

a wind has blown the rain away and blown
the sky away and all the leaves away,
and the trees stand.   I think i too have known
autumn too long

               (and what have you to say,
wind wind wind—did you love somebody
and have you the petal of somewhere in your heart
pinched from dumb summer?
                  O crazy daddy
of death dance cruelly for us and start

the last leaf whirling in the final brain
of air!)Let us as we have seen see
doom's integration.........a wind has blown the rain

away and the leaves and the sky and the
trees stand:
           the trees stand.   The trees,
suddenly wait against the moon's face.

SONNETS—ACTUALITIES

I

when my love comes to see me it's
just a little like music,a
little more like curving colour(say
orange)
         against silence,or darkness....

the coming of my love emits
a wonderful smell in my mind,

you should see when i turn to find
her how my least heart-beat becomes less.
And then all her beauty is a vise

whose stilling lips murder suddenly me,

but of my corpse the tool her smile makes something
suddenly luminous and precise

—and then we are I and She....

what is that the hurdy-gurdy's playing

II

it is funny,you will be dead some day.
By you the mouth hair eyes,and i mean
the unique and nervously obscene

need;it's funny.   They will all be dead

knead of lustfulhunched deeplytoplay
lips and stare the gross fuzzy-pash
—dead—and the dark gold delicately smash....
grass,and the stars,of my shoulder in stead.

It is a funny,thing.   And you will be

and i and all the days and nights that matter
knocked by sun moon jabbed jerked with ecstasy
....tremble(not knowing how much better

than me will you like the rain's face and

the rich improbable hands of the Wind)

III

i have loved,let us see if that's all.
Bit into you as teeth,in the stone
of a musical fruit.   My lips pleasantly groan
on your taste.   Jumped the quick wall

of your smile into stupid gardens
if this were not enough(not really enough
pulled one before one the vague tough

exquisite

      flowers,whom hardens
richly,darkness.   On the whole
possibly have i loved....?you)
                   sheath before sheath

stripped to the Odour.   (and here's what WhoEver will know
Had you as bite teeth;
i stood with you as a foal

stands but as the trees,lay,which grow

IV

      the mind is its own beautiful prisoner.
Mine looked long at the sticky moon
opening in dusk her new wings

then decently hanged himself,one afternoon.

The last thing he saw was you
naked amid unnaked things,

your flesh,a succinct wandlike animal,
a little strolling with the futile purr
of blood;your sex squeaked like a billiard–cue
chalking itself,as not to make an error,
with twists spontaneously methodical.
He suddenly tasted worms windows and roses

he laughed,and closed his eyes as a girl closes
her left hand upon a mirror.

V

even a pencil has fear to
do the posed body luckily made
a pen is dreadfully afraid
of her of this of the smile's two
eyes....too,since the world's but
a piece of eminent fragility.
Well and when—Does susceptibility
imply perspicuity,or?
                              shut
up.
        Seeing
                    seeing her is not
to something or to nothing as much as
being by her seen,which has got
nothing on something as i think

,did you ever hear a jazz
Band?

        or unnoise men don't make soup who drink.

VI

let's live suddenly without thinking

under honest trees,
                    a stream
does.the brain of cleverly–crinkling
–water pursues the angry dream
of the shore.   By midnight,
                         a moon
scratches the skin of the organised hills

an edged nothing begins to prune

let's live like the light that kills
and let's as silence,
                    because Whirl's after all:
(after me)love,and after you.
I occasionally feel vague how
vague i don't know tenuous Now-
spears and The Then-arrows making do
our mouths something red,something tall

VII

yours is the music for no instrument
yours the preposterous colour unbeheld

—mine the unbought contemptuous intent
till this our flesh merely shall be excelled
by speaking flower
                    (if i have made songs

it does not greatly matter to the sun,
nor will rain care

> cautiously who prolongs
unserious twilight)Shadows have begun

the hair's worm huge,ecstatic,rathe....

yours are the poems i do not write.

In this at least we have got a bulge on death,
silence,and the keenly musical light

of sudden nothing....la bocca mia "he
kissed wholly trembling"

> or so thought the lady.

VIII

fabulous against   ,a,fathoming jelly
of vital futile huge light as she
does not stand-ing.unsits

> her(wrist
performs a thundering trivial)it.y

protuberant through the room's skilful of thing
silent spits discrete lumps of noise....
furniture

> unsolemnly   :bur   sting
the skinfull of Ludicrous,solidity which a.   ,kissed
with is nearness.(peers:body of

                              aching toys
in unsmooth sexual luminosity spree.

—dear)the   uncouthly Her.thuglike stare the
pollenizing vacancy
when,Thy patters?hands....is swig

it does who eye   sO neatly big

                    IX

by little accurate saints thickly which tread
the serene nervous light of paradise—
by angelfaces clustered like bright lice

about god's capable dull important head—
by on whom glories whisperingly impinge
(god's pretty mother)but may not confuse

the clever hair nor rout the young mouth whose
lips begin a smile exactly strange—
this painter should have loved my lady.
And by this throat a little suddenly lifted

in singing—hands fragile whom almost tire
the sleepshaped lilies—

                         should my lady's body
with these frail ladies dangerously respire:

impeccable girls in raiment laughter-gifted.

X

a thing most new complete fragile intense,
which wholly trembling memory undertakes
—your kiss,the little pushings of flesh,makes
my body sorry when the minute moon
is a remarkable splinter in the quick
of twilight
            ....or if sunset utters one
unhurried muscled huge chromatic
fist skilfully modeling silence
—to feel how through the stopped entire day
horribly and seriously thrills
the moment of enthusiastic space
is a little wonderful,and say
Perhaps her body touched me;and to face

suddenly the lighted living hills

XI

autumn is:that between there and here
gladness flays hideously hills.
It was in the spring of this very year

(a spring of wines women and window-sills)
i met that hideous gladness,per the face
—pinxit,who knows?   Who knows?   Some "allemand"....?
of Goethe,since exempt from heaven's grace,

in an engraving belonging to my friend.
Whom i salute,by what is dear to us;

and by a gestured city stilled in the framing
twilight of Spring....and the dream of dreaming
—and i fall back,quietly amorous
of,through the autumn indisputably roaming

death's big rotten particular kiss.

XII

my love is building a building
around you,a frail slippery
house,a strong fragile house
(beginning at the singular beginning

of your smile)a skilful uncouth
prison,a precise clumsy
prison(building thatandthis into Thus,
Around the reckless magic of your mouth)

my love is building a magic,a discrete
tower of magic and(as i guess)

when Farmer Death(whom fairies hate)shall

crumble the mouth-flower fleet
He'll not my tower,
                          laborious,casual

where the surrounded smile
                                        hangs

                                                  breathless

XIII

perhaps it is to feel strike
the silver fish of her nakedness
with fins sharply pleasant,my

youth has travelled toward her these years

or to snare the timid like
of her mind to my mind that i

am come by little countries to the yes

of her youth.
     And if somebody hears
what i say—let him be pitiful:
because i've travelled all alone
through the forest of wonderful,
and that my feet have surely known
the furious ways and the peaceful,

and because she is beautiful

XIV

the ivory performing rose

of you,worn upon my mind
all night,quitting only in the unkind

dawn its muscle amorous

pricks with minute odour these gross
days
     when i think of you and do not live:
and the empty twilight cannot grieve
nor the autumn,as i grieve,faint for your face

O stay with me slightly.   or until

with neat obscure obvious hands

Time stuff the sincere stomach of each mill

of the ingenious gods.(i am punished.
They have stolen into recent lands
the flower
        with their enormous fingers unwished

XV

my naked lady framed
in twilight is an accident

whose niceness betters easily the intent
of genius—
       painting wholly feels ashamed
before this music,and poetry cannot
go near because perfectly fearful.

meanwhile these speak her wonderful
But i(having in my arms caught

the picture)hurry it slowly

to my mouth,taste the accurate demure
ferocious
           rhythm of
                   precise
laziness.   Eat the price

of an imaginable gesture

exact warm unholy

XVI

i have found what you are like
the rain,

     (Who feathers frightened fields
with the superior dust-of-sleep. wields

easily the pale club of the wind
and swirled justly souls of flower strike

the air in utterable coolness

deeds of green thrilling light
                  with thinned
newfragile yellows

           lurch and.press
—in the woods
        which
           stutter
              and

                  sing

And the coolness of your smile is
stirringofbirds between my arms;but
i should rather than anything
have(almost when hugeness will shut
quietly)almost,
                          your kiss

XVII

                    —GON splashes-sink
which is east eighth,a star of three annoys

me,but the stink of perfumed noise
fiercely mounts from the fireman's ball,i think

and also i think of you,getting mandolin–clink
mixed with your hair;feeling your knees
among the supercilious chimneys,

my nerves sumptuously wink
....and little-dusk has his toys to play with
windows-and-whispers,
                              (will BigMorning get away with
them?j'm'en doute,)
                    chérie,j'm'en doute.

the accurate key to a palace

—You,—in this window sits a Face
(it is twilight)a Face playing on a flute

XVIII

my sonnet is A light goes on in
the toiletwindow,that's straightacross from
my window,night air bothered with a rustling din

sort of sublimated tom-tom
which quite outdoes the mandolin-

man's tiny racket.   The horses sleep upstairs.
And you can see their ears.   Ears win-

k,funny stable.   In the morning they go out in pairs:
amazingly,one pair is white
(but you know that)they look at each other.   Nudge.

(if they love each other,who cares?)
They pull the morning out of the night.

I am living with a mouse who shares

my meals with him,which is fair as i judge.

XIX

(the phonograph's voice like a keen spider skipping

quickly over patriotic swill.
The,negress,in the,rocker by the,curb,tipping

and tipping,the flocks of pigeons.   And the skil-

ful loneliness,and the rather fat
man in bluishsuspenders half-reading the
Evening Something
                              in the normal window.   and a cat.

A cat waiting for god knows makes me

wonder if i'm alive(eye pries,

not open.   Tail stirs.)   And the. fire-escapes—
the night. makes me wonder if,if i am
the face of a baby smeared with beautiful jam

or

my invincible Nearness rapes

laughter from your preferable,eyes

you asked me to come:it was raining a little,
and the spring;a clumsy brightness of air
wonderfully stumbled above the square,
little amorous-tadpole people wiggled

battered by stuttering pearl,
                                            leaves jiggled
to the jigging fragrance of newness
—and then.   My crazy fingers liked your dress
....your kiss,your kiss was a distinct brittle

flower,and the flesh crisp set
my love-tooth on edge.   So until light
each having each we promised to forget—

wherefore is there nothing left to guess:
the cheap intelligent thighs,the electric trite
thighs;the hair stupidly priceless.

XXI

(let us tremble)a personal radiance sits
hideously upon the trafficking hum
of dusk
      each street takes of shadowy
light the droll snowing delirium

(we do not speak)
            tumbled hushingly bits
of downward flower flowing without or cease

or time;a naming stealth of ecstasy
means,like a girl lasciviously frail,
                 peace
(dreaming is better)

         murdering coolness slowly
in peopling places seeks play:withs of star
link clauses of warmth
        (after dream who knows?)
a blackish cat and a bluish cat are

eyeing,as with almost melancholy
delicacy night gargles windows.

XXII

utterly and amusingly i am pash
possibly because
        .dusk and if it
perhaps drea-mingly Is(not-
quite trees hugging with the rash,

coherent light
)only to trace with
stiffening slow shrill eyes beyond a fit-
and-cling of stuffs the alert willing myth
of body,which will make oddly to strut
my indolent priceless smile,
                                until
this very frail enormous star(do you see
it?)and this shall dance upon the nude
and final silence and shall the
(i do but touch you)timid lewd
moon plunge skilfully into the hill.

XXIII

notice the convulsed orange inch of moon
perching on this silver minute of evening.

We'll choose the way to the forest—no offense
to you,white town whose spires softly dare.
Will take the houseless wisping rune
of road lazily carved on sharpening air.

Fields lying miraculous in violent silence

fill with microscopic whithering
...(that's the Black People,chérie,
who live under stones.) Don't be afraid

and we will pass the simple ugliness
of exact tombs,where a large road crosses
and all the people are minutely dead.

Then you will slowly kiss me

XXIV

and this day it was Spring....us
drew lewdly the murmurous minute clumsy
smelloftheworld.   We intricately
alive,cleaving the luminous stammer of bodies
(eagerly just not each other touch)seeking,some
street which easily tickles a brittle fuss
of fragile huge humanity....
                                        Numb
thoughts,kicking in the rivers of our blood,miss
by how terrible inches speech—it
made you a little dizzy did the world's smell
(but i was thinking why the girl-and-bird
of you move....moves....and also,i'll admit—)

till,at the corner of Nothing and Something,we heard
a handorgan in twilight playing like hell

&
[AND]

To
E. O.

A

POST IMPRESSIONS

I

the wind is a Lady with
bright slender eyes(who

moves)at sunset
and who—touches—the
hills without any reason

(i have spoken with this
indubitable and green person "Are
You the wind?" "Yes" "why do you touch flowers
as if they were unalive,as

if They were ideas?" "because,sir
things which in my mind blossom will
stumble beneath a clumsiest disguise,appear
capable of fragility and indecision

—do not suppose these
without any reason and otherwise
roses and mountains
different from the i am who wanders

imminently across the renewed world"
to me said the)wind being A lady in a green
dress,who;touches:the fields
(at sunset)

II

Take for example this:

if to the colour of midnight
to a more than darkness(which
is myself and Paris and all
things)the bright
rain
occurs deeply,beautifully

and i(being at a window
in this midnight)
                    for no reason feel
deeply completely conscious of the rain or rather
Somebody who uses roofs and streets skilfully to make a
possible and beautiful sound:

if a(perhaps)clock strikes,in the alive
coolness,very faintly and
finally through altogether delicate gestures of rain

a colour comes,which is morning,O do not wonder that

(just at the edge of day)i surely
make a millionth poem which will not wholly
miss you;or if i certainly create,lady,
one of the thousand selves who are your smile.

III

Paris;this April sunset completely utters
utters serenely silently a cathedral

before whose upward lean magnificent face
the streets turn young with rain,

spiral acres of bloated rose
coiled within cobalt miles of sky
yield to and heed
the mauve
            of twilight(who slenderly descends,
daintily carrying in her eyes the dangerous first stars)
people move love hurry in a gently

arriving gloom and
see!(the new moon
fills abruptly with sudden silver
these torn pockets of lame and begging colour)while
there and here the lithe indolent prostitute
Night,argues

with certain houses

IV

I remark this beach has been used too.   much Too.   originally
spontaneous twurls-of-excrement inanely codified with superb
sunlight,   jolts of delapidation bath-houses whose opened
withins ejaculate. obscenity   the tide Did dl es a,fad ed
explosion of, pink!stocking

w h e e saysthesea-brE aking-b Re   akin g(brea)K   ing

my Nose puts on sharp robes of uncouth odour,for an onion!for
one—onion for.   putrescence is Cubical   sliced-nicelybits
Of,   shivers ofcrin Ging stink.dull, globular glows and
flatchatte ringarom a .s

—w hee e;

seasays Break snice-Ly in-twin K les Of,CleaN

a booming smell waddles toward,me,dressed like a Plum grinning
softly,New   focus-of disintegrat i o n ?   my

mind laughsin- to Slivers of (unthinking.c'est

l'heure

      exquise)i remind Me of HerThe delicate-swill tints of

hair Whose(the lit-tle m-oo-n' s o u t)   flesh   stalks
the Momentinmyarms

your expression
          my love
             when most passionate.,

                        my,love
is thatofa fly.pre cisel Yhalf

(squashe)d

      with,its,little,solemn,   entrails

         V

      my smallheaded pearshaped

      lady in gluey twilight
      moving,suddenly

      is three animals.   The
      minute waist continually

      with an African gesture

utters a frivolous intense half of
Girl which(like some

floating snake upon itself always and
slowly which upward certainly is pouring)emits
a pose
        :to twitter wickedly

whereas the big and firm legs moving solemnly
like careful and furious and beautiful elephants

(mingled in whispering thickly smooth thighs
thinkingly)
remind me of Woman and

how between
her hips India is.

VI

of this sunset(which is so
filled with fear people bells)i
say your eyes can take
day away more softly horribly suddenly;

(of these two most
early stars wincing upon a single
colour,i know only that your hands
move more simply upon the evening

and à propos such light and shape as means
the moon,i somehow feel
your smile slightly is a more
minute adventure)

lady.   The clumsy dark threatens(and i do
not speak nor think nor am aware
of anything
                    save that these houses bulge
like memories in one crooked street

of a mind peacefully and skilfully which is disappearing

VII

my eyes are fond of the east side
as i lie asleep my eyes go into Allen street the dark long cool tunnel
of raving colour,on either side the windows are packed with hardslippery
greens and helplessbaby blues and stic-ky chromes and prettylemons and
virginal pinks and wealthy vermilion and breathless-scarlet,dark colours
like 'cellos keen fiddling colours colours cOOler than harps colours
p r i c k i n glike piccolos thumPing colours like a bangofpiano colours
which,are,the,flowery pluckings of a harpsichord colours of Pure percus-
sion colours-like-trumpets they(writhe they,struggleinweird chords of
humorous,fury heapingandsqueezing tum-bling-scratchingcrowd ingworming
each by screeching Each)on either side the street's DarkcOOllonGBody
windows,are. clenched. fistsoftint.
            TUMTITUMTIDDLE
if sometimes my eyes stay at home
then my mouth will go out into the East side,my mouth goes to the peddlers,
to the peddlers of smooth,fruits of eager colours of the little,huddling
nuts and the bad candies my,mouth loves melons slitted with bright knives,
it stains itself,with currants and cherries it (swallow s bun chesofnew
grapes likeGree n A r e b u b b l e s asc end-ing inthecarts my,mouth
is,fond of tiny plums of tangerines and apples it will,Gorge indistinct
palishflesh of laZilytas tingg OO seberries,it,loves these better than,
cubesandovalsof sweetness but it swallow) s greedily sugaredellipses it
does not disdain picKles,once,it,ate a scarlet pepper and my eyes were
buttoned with pain
            THE BLACK CAT WITH
is there anything my ears love it's

to go into the east Side in a. dark street a hurDygurdY with thequeer
hopping ghosts of children.   my,ears know the fuZZy tune that's played
by the Funny hand of the paralyticwhose dod d e rin g partner whEEl
shi min chb yi nch along the whirlingPeaceful furious street people
drop,coppers into,the littletin-cup His wrappedupbody Queerly Has,my,
ears,go into Hassan's place the kanoonchir p ing the bigtwittering
zither-and the mealy,ladies dancing thicklyfoolish,with,the,tam,bou,
rine,s And the violin spitting squeakysongs into the cuspidor-col our-
edRoom and,my ears bend to the little silent handorgan propping the
curve of the tiny motheaten old manwhose Beard rests.onthetopwhose
silly,Hand revolves,perfectly,slowlywith,the handle ofa crankin It
The L's roar tortures-pleasantly myears it is,like the,Jab:of a dark
tool.   With a cleverjeRk in itlike the motionofa Sharp Knife-sN ap-
pingof fadeadf ish' shead Or,the whipping of a blackSnake cu tSudden ly
in 2 that,writhes...A..lit.tleora basket of RipeBlackbeRRies emptied
suddenl (y down the squirming sPine of the)unsuspecting street;
                    THE YELLOW EYES AND
—;i Like to
Lie On My Couch at Christopher Street For my stomach goes out into The
east side my sex sitting upright on the stomach like A billiken with
hisknees huggedtogether it,goes out into the rapid hard women and
intotheslow hot women   my Stomach ruBSiTSElf kew-re-ous-ly a mong
Them(among their stomachs andtheir sexes   )stomachsofold pe o pleLike
hideous vegetaBles weazEned with-being-put-too-long in windows and
never sold and couldn't-be-given-away because Who?wanted them,stom-
achslikEDead fishe s s olemnandputrid vast,stomachs bLurting and
cHuckling like uninteresting-landscapes made interesting by earTHQuake
empty stomachsClenche Dtothe beautiful-curveofhunger, cHuBbY stomachs
which have not,known other stomachs and their Sexis a Lone ly,flower
whose secretloveliness hur.ts itse;l.f to no-thing   signifi-cant
stomachs:Who carry-tadpole!s,,stomachs of little,girls smoothanduseless
i,like,best,the,stomachs,of the young (girls silky and lewd)like corn
s l e n derl y tottering in sun-light
                    THE
nobody(knows and WhoEver would)?dance lewd dollies pretty and putrid
dollies of-love-and-of-death dollies of perfect life,

dollies of anyway
        VIOLIN

VIII

suppose
Life is an old man carrying flowers on his head.

young death sits in a café
smiling,a piece of money held between
his thumb and first finger

(i say "will he buy flowers" to you
and "Death is young
life wears velour trousers
life totters,life has a beard" i

say to you who are silent.—"Do you see
Life?he is there and here,
or that,or this
or nothing or an old man 3 thirds
asleep,on his head
flowers,always crying
to nobody something about les
roses les bluets
               yes,
                   will He buy?
Les belles bottes—oh hear
,pas chères")

and my love slowly answered I think so.   But
I think I see someone else

there is a lady,whose name is Afterwards
she is sitting beside young death,is slender;
likes flowers.

PORTRAITS

I

when the spent day begins to frail
(whose grave already three or two
young stars with spades of silver dig)

by beauty i declare to you

if what i am at one o'clock
to little lips(which have not sinned
in whose displeasure lives a kiss)
kneeling,your frequent mercy begs,

sharply believe me,wholly,well
—did(wisely suddenly into
a dangerous womb of cringing air)
the largest hour push deep his din

of wallowing male(shock beyond shock
blurted)strokes,vibrant with the purr
of echo pouring in a mesh
of following tone:did this and this

spire strike midnight(and did occur
bell beyond fiercely spurting bell
a jetted music splashing fresh
upon silence)i without fail

entered became and was these twin
imminent lisping bags of flesh;
became eyes moist lithe shuddering big,
the luminous laughter,and the legs

whereas,at twenty minutes to

one,i am this blueeyed Finn
emerging from a lovehouse who
buttons his coat against the wind

||

impossibly

motivated by midnight
the flyspecked abdominous female
indubitably tellurian
strolls
        emitting minute grins

each an intaglio.
Nothing
has also carved upon her much

too white forehead a pair of
eyes which mutter thickly(as one merely
terricolous American an instant doubts
the authenticity

of these antiquities—relaxing
                                    hurries
 elsewhere;to blow

incredible wampum

III

here is little Effie's head
whose brains are made of gingerbread
when the judgment day comes
God will find six crumbs

stooping by the coffinlid
waiting for something to rise
as the other somethings did—
you imagine His surprise

bellowing through the general noise
Where is Effie who was dead?
—to God in a tiny voice,
i am may the first crumb said

whereupon its fellow five
crumbs chuckled as if they were alive
and number two took up the song,
might i'm called and did no wrong

cried the third crumb,i am should
and this is my little sister could
with our big brother who is would
don't punish us for we were good;

and the last crumb with some shame
whispered unto God,my name
is must and with the others i've
been Effie who isn't alive

just imagine it I say
God amid a monstrous din
watch your step and follow me
stooping by Effie's little,in

(want a match or can you see?)
which the six subjunctive crumbs

twitch like mutilated thumbs:
picture His peering biggest whey

coloured face on which a frown
puzzles,but I know the way—
(nervously Whose eyes approve
the blessed while His ears are crammed

with the strenous music of
the innumerable capering damned)
—staring wildly up and down
and here we are now judgment day

cross the threshold have no dread
lift the sheet back in this way.
here is little Effie's head
whose brains are made of gingerbread

N

&:SEVEN POEMS

I

                              i will be
M o ving in the Street of her

bodyfee l inga ro undMe the traffic of
lovely;muscles-sinke x p i r i n   g S
      uddenl
Y   totouch
                    the curvedship of
                              Her-
....kIss   her:hands
                    will play on,mE as
dea d tunes OR s–crap p–y lea Ves flut te rin g
from Hideous trees or

      Maybe Mandolins
                    l oo k-
      pigeons fly ingand

whee(:are,SpRiN,k,LiNg an in-stant with sunLight
then)l-
ing all go BlacK wh–eel–ing

oh
   ver
      mYveRylitTle

street
where

you will come,

                            at twi li ght
            s(oon & there's
            a   m oo
)n.

                            ||

i'll tell you a dream i had once i was away up in the sky Blue,everything:
a bar the bar was made of brass hangIng from strings (or)someThing i was
lying on the bar it was cOOl i didn't have anything on and I was hot all
Hot and the bar was

        COOl
O My lover,

                there's just room for me in You
my stomach goes into your Little Stomach My legs are in your legs Your
arms
        under me around; my head fits(my head)in your Brain—my,head's
big
she(said laughing
)with your head.all big

                            |||

                Spring is like a perhaps hand
                (which comes carefully
                out of Nowhere)arranging
                a window,into which people look(while

people stare
arranging and changing placing
carefully there a strange
thing and a known thing here)and

changing everything carefully

spring is like a perhaps
Hand in a window
(carefully to
and fro moving New and
Old things,while
people stare carefully
moving a perhaps
fraction of flower here placing
an inch of air there)and

without breaking anything.

IV

Who
  threw the silver dollar up into the tree?

         I didn't said the little
lady who sews and grows every day paler-paler she sits sewing and grow-
ing and that's the truth,
who threw

    the ripe melon into the tree?you
          got me said the smoke who
runs the elevator but I bet two bits come seven come eleven mm make
the world safe for democracy it never fails and that's a fact;

who threw the

bunch of violets

             into the tree?I dunno said the silver dog,   with ripe
eyes and wagged his tail that's the god's own

and the moon kissed the little lady on her paler-paler face and said
never mind,you'll find

             But the moon creeped into the pink hand of the
smoke that shook the ivories

              and she said said She Win and you won't be

sorry   And The Moon came!along-along to the waggy silver dog
and the moon came
and the Moon said into his Ripe Eyes

              and the moon

                  Smiled

                ,so

            V

gee i like to think of dead it means nearer because deeper firmer
since darker than little round water at one end of the well   it's
too cool to be crooked and it's too firm to be hard but it's sharp
and thick and it loves,   every old thing falls in rosebugs and
jackknives and kittens and pennies they all sit there looking at
each other having the fastest time because they've never met before

dead's more even than how many ways of sitting on your head your
unnatural hair has in the morning

dead's clever too like POF goes the alarm off and the little striker
having the best time tickling away everybody's brain so everybody
just puts out their finger and they stuff the poor thing all full
of fingers

dead has a smile like the nicest man you've never met who maybe winks
at you in a streetcar and you pretend you don't but really you do
see and you are My how glad he winked and hope he'll do it again

or if it talks about you somewhere behind your back it makes your neck
feel pleasant and stoopid   and if dead says may i have this one and
was never introduced you say Yes because you know you want it to dance
with you and it wants to and it can dance and Whocares

dead's fine like hands do you see that water flowerpots in windows but
they live higher in their house than you so that's all you see but you
don't want to

dead's happy like the way underclothes All so differently solemn and
inti and sitting on one string

dead never says my dear, Time for your musiclesson and you like music
and to have somebody play who can but you know you never can and why
have to?

dead's nice like a dance where you danced simple hours and you take all
your prickly-clothes off and squeeze-into-largeness without one word   and
you lie still as anything   in largeness and this largeness begins to give
you,the dance all over again and you,feel all again all over the way men
you liked made you feel when they touched you(but that's not all)because
largeness tells you so you can feel what you made,men feel when,you
touched, them

dead's sorry like a thistlefluff-thing which goes landing away all by
himself on somebody's roof or something where who-ever-heard-of-
growing and nobody expects you to anyway

dead says come with me he says(andwhyevernot)into the round well and
see the kitten and the penny and the jackknife and the rosebug
                                                        and you
say Sure you say   (like that)   sure i'll come with you you say for i
like kittens i do and jackknives i do and pennies i do and rosebugs i do

VI

(one!)

the wisti–twisti barber
-pole is climbing

people high,up–in

tenements talk.in sawdust Voices

                              a:whispering drunkard passes

VII

who knows if the moon's
a balloon,coming out of a keen city
in the sky—filled with pretty people?
(and if you and i should

get into it,if they
should take me and take you into their balloon,
why then
we'd go up higher with all the pretty people

than houses and steeples and clouds:
go sailing
away and away sailing into a keen
city which nobody's ever visited,where

always
          it's
                  Spring)and everyone's
in love and flowers pick themselves

D

SONNETS—REALITIES

I

O It's Nice To Get Up In,the slipshod mucous kiss
of her riant belly's fooling bore
—When The Sun Begins To(with a phrasing crease
of hot subliminal lips,as if a score
of youngest angels suddenly should stretch neat necks
just to see how always squirms
the skilful mystery of Hell)me suddenly

grips in chuckles of supreme sex.

In The Good Old Summer Time.
My gorgeous bullet in tickling intuitive flight
aches,just,simply,into,her.   Thirsty
stirring. (Must be summer. Hush. Worms.)
But It's Nicer To Lie In Bed
                              —eh?   I'm

not.   Again.   Hush.   God.   Please hold.   Tight

II

     my strength becoming wistful in a glib

     girl i consider her as a leaf
               thinks
     of the sky,my mind takes to nib
     -bling,of her posture.   (As an eye winks).

     and almost i refrain from jumbling her

flesh whose casual mouth's coy rooting
dies also.   (my loveFist in her knuckling

thighs,
        with a sharp indecent stir
unclenches

                into fingers....she too is tired.
Not of me.   The eyes which biggish loll

the hands' will tumbling into shall

—and Love 's a coach with gilt hopeless wheels mired
where sits rigidly her body's doll
gay exactly perishing sexual,

III

    the dirty colours of her kiss have just
throttled
            my seeing blood,her heart's chatter

riveted a weeping skyscraper

in me

        i bite on the eyes' brittle crust
(only feeling the belly's merry thrust
Boost my huge passion like a business

and the Y her legs panting as they press

proffers its omelet of fluffy lust)
at six exactly
            the alarm tore

two slits in her cheeks.   A brain peered at the dawn.
she got up

              with a gashing yellow yawn
and tottered to a glass bumping things.
she picked wearily something from the floor

Her hair was mussed,and she coughed while tying strings

                         IV

      light cursed falling in a singular block
      her,rain-warm-naked
                              exquisitely hashed

      (little careful hunks-of-lilac laughter splashed
      from the world prettily upward,mock
      us....)
                   and there was a clock.   tac-tic.   tac-toc.

      Time and lilacs....minutes and love....do you?and
      always
              (i simply understand
      the gnashing petals of sex which lock
      me seriously.

                         Dumb for a while.my

      god—a patter of kisses,the chewed stump

      of a mouth,huge dropping of a flesh from
      hinging thighs
                      ....merci....i want to die
      nous sommes heureux

My soul a limp lump

of lymph
      she kissed
           and i

                ....chéri....nous sommes

V

the bed is not very big

a sufficient pillow shoveling
her small manure-shaped head

one sheet on which distinctly wags

at times the weary twig
of a neckless nudity
(very occasionally budding

a flabby algebraic odour

jigs
    et tout en face
always wiggles the perfectly dead
finger of thitherhithering gas.

clothed with a luminous fur

poilu

    a Jesus sags
in frolicsome wooden agony).

VI

the poem her belly marched through me as
one army.　From her nostrils to her feet

she smelled of silence.　The inspired cleat

of her glad leg pulled into a sole mass
my separate lusts
　　　　　　　her hair was like a gas
evil to feel.　Unwieldy....

　　　　　　　　the bloodbeat
in her fierce laziness tried to repeat
a trick of syncopation Europe has

—. One day i felt a mountain touch me where
i stood (maybe nine miles off).　It was spring

sun-stirring.　sweetly to the mangling air
muchness of buds mattered.　a valley spilled
its tickling river in my eyes,
　　　　　　　　the killed

world wriggled like a twitched string.

VII

an amiable putrescence carpenters

the village of her mind bodily which

ravelling,to a proud continual stitch
of the unmitigated sistole

                        purrs
against my mind,the eyes' shuddering burrs
of light stick on my brain harder than can twitch
its terrors;
                the,mouth's,swallowed,muscle(itch
of groping mucous)in my mouth occurs

homelessly.   While grip Hips simply.   well
fussed flesh does surely to mesh.   New
and eager.   wittily peels the.   ploop.—OOc h get:breath
once,all over,kid how,funny Do tell
....sweat,succeeds breathings stopped
                                        to

hear,in darkness,water the lips of death

VIII

    her careful distinct sex whose sharp lips comb

    my mumbling gropeofstrength(staggered by the lug
    of love)
            sincerely greets,with an occult shrug
    asking Through her Muteness will slowly roam
    my dumbNess?

                    her other,wet,warm

    lips limp,across my bruising smile;
    as rapidly upon the jiggled norm

    of agony my grunting eyes pin tailored flames
    Her being at this instant commits

    an impenetrable transparency.
    the harsh erecting breasts and uttering tits

punish my hug
         presto!

               the bright rile
of jovial hair extremely frames

the face in a hoop of grim ecstasy

IX

in making Marjorie god hurried
a boy's body on unsuspicious
legs of girl. his left hand quarried
the quartzlike face. his right slapped
the amusing big vital vicious
vegetable of her mouth.
Upon the whole he suddenly clapped
a tiny sunset of vermouth
-colour. Hair. he put between
her lips a moist mistake,whose fragrance hurls
me into tears,as the dusty new-
ness of her obsolete gaze begins to. lean....
a little against me,when for two
dollars i fill her hips with boys and girls

SONNETS—ACTUALITIES

I

before the fragile gradual throne of night
slowly when several stars are opening
one beyond one immaculate curving
cool treasures of silence

                (slenderly wholly
rising,herself uprearing wholly slowly,
lean in the hips and her sails filled with dream—
when on a green brief gesture of twilight
trembles the imagined galleon of Spring)

somewhere unspeaking sits my life;the grim
clenched mind of me somewhere begins again,
shares the year's perfect agony.   Waiting

(always)upon a fragile instant when

herself me(slowly,wholly me)will press
in the young lips unearthly slenderness

II

when i have thought of you somewhat too
much and am become perfectly and
simply Lustful....sense a gradual stir
of beginning muscle,and what it will do
to me before shutting....understand
i love you....feel your suddenly body reach
for me with a speed of white speech

(the simple instant of perfect hunger
Yes)
     how beautifully swims
the fooling world in my huge blood,
cracking brains A swiftlyenormous light
—and furiously puzzling through,prismatic,whims,
the chattering self perceives with hysterical fright

a comic tadpole wriggling in delicious mud

III

if i should sleep with a lady called death
get another man with firmer lips
to take your new mouth in his teeth
(hips pumping pleasure into hips).

Seeing how the limp huddling string
of your smile over his body squirms
kissingly,i will bring you every spring
handfuls of little normal worms.

Dress deftly your flesh in stupid stuffs,
phrase the immense weapon of your hair.
Understanding why his eye laughs,
i will bring you every year

something which is worth the whole,
an inch of nothing for your soul.

IV

upon the room's
              silence,i will sew

a nagging button of candlelight
(halfstooping to exactly kiss the trite

worm of her nakedness
                      until it go

rapidly to bed:i will get in with
it,wisely,pester skilfully,teasing

its lips,absurd eyes,the hair).   Creasing
its smoothness—and leave the bed agrin with

memories
         (this white worm and i who

love to feel what it will do
in my bullying fingers)
as for the candle,it'll

turn into a little curse

of wax.   Something,distinct and.   Amusing,brittle

V

        a blue woman with sticking out breasts hanging
clothes.   On the line. not so old
for the mother of twelve undershirts(we are told
by is it Bishop Taylor who needs hanging

that marriage is a sure cure for masturbation).

        A dirty wind,twitches the,clothes which are clean
—this is twilight,
        a little puppy hopping between
skipping
    children
        (It is the consummation
of day,the hour)she says to me you big fool
she says i says to her i says Sally
i says
    the

mmmoon,begins to,drool

softly,in the hot alley,

a nigger's voice feels curiously cool
(suddenly-Lights go!on,by schedule

VI

when you went away it was morning
(that is,big horses;light feeling up
streets;heels taking derbies (where?) a pup
hurriedly hunched over swill;one butting

trolley imposingly empty;snickering
shop doors unlocked by white–grub
faces) clothes in delicate hubbub

as you stood thinking of anything,

maybe the world....But i have wondered since
isn't it odd of you really to lie
a sharp agreeable flower between my

amused legs
                    kissing with little dints

of april,making the obscene shy
breasts tickle,laughing when i wilt and wince

VII

i like my body when it is with your
body.   It is so quite new a thing.
Muscles better and nerves more.
i like your body.   i like what it does,
i like its hows.   i like to feel the spine
of your body and its bones,and the trembling
-firm-smooth ness and which i will
again and again and again
kiss,   i like kissing this and that of you,
i like,slowly stroking the,shocking fuzz
of your electric fur,and what-is-it comes
over parting flesh....And eyes big love-crumbs,

and possibly i like the thrill

of under me you so quite new

AFTERWORD

by
George James Firmage

The publishing history of *Tulips & Chimneys*, which Richard Kennedy has described in his Introduction to this volume, is mirrored in the state of the four surviving copies of E. E. Cummings' manuscript. None of them has been correctly identified or cataloged. The earliest copy, now in the Dial Collection in the Beinecke Rare Book and Manuscript Library, Yale University, is simply labeled "Typewritten ms . . . from which poems for publication in *The Dial* were selected."[1] The reference to *The Dial* is certainly true, for the copy of *Tulips & Chimneys* which the poet prepared during the final months of 1919 and gave to his friend, Stewart Mitchell, the magazine's first managing editor, early in January 1920, was used for that purpose after Mitchell had failed to find a publisher for the manuscript as a whole.[2] Unfortunately, the copy at Yale is incomplete. But even in its present form, it clearly establishes the fact that at least 17 of the 34 poems added to *&* were part of the original manuscript and that most, if not all, of the poems that appeared in *Tulips and Chimneys* (1923), *&* (1925) and *XLI Poems* (1925) were written before 1920.

The other copies of the manuscript, which Cummings re-

1. Za *Dial*.
2. According to Charles Norman, Mitchell told him "that, beginning in January, 1920, he took the original manuscript of *Tulips and Chimneys* to five publishers, all of whom declined it. . . ." *The Magic-Maker: E. E. Cummings* (New York: The Macmillan Company, 1958), pp. 156–157.

vised in Paris between June 1921 and February 1922 and gave to John Dos Passos to see "publishers to Hell in my behalf anent some poems,"[3] form the basis of the present edition of the work. The two copies in the "Papers of Edward Estlin Cummings" in the Houghton Library, Harvard University, are cataloged as "[Tulips and chimneys] ... Copies of poems,"[4] "[Tulips and chimneys] ... Divisional titles,"[5] "[Tulips and chimneys: poems omitted from the original edition]"[6] and "[And] ... Copies of poems."[7] The remaining copy in the University of Texas Humanities Research Center, Austin, is listed under "[Xli poems]" and "[Tulips and chimneys]."[8] All of the manuscripts are incomplete. The two Harvard copies contain 147 of the 152 poems between them; 42 of these are held in common. The Texas copy contains only 32 poems, all of them present in the other copies; but the poems are consecutive from "Epithalamion" to "Amores" IX and confirm, at least in part, the order of the poems in the Harvard version. All together there are five poems missing. However, individual typescripts for four of the poems are also in the Houghton collection and these are the versions that appear here.[9] The fifth poem, "Picasso," is a reconstruction.

The two typescripts at Harvard were uncovered by the present writer as the result of a detailed examination and reclassification of the catalog material noted above. One is a

3. From a letter to his mother, February 1922, in *Selected Letters of E. E. Cummings* (New York: Harcourt Brace Jovanovich, 1969), p. 83.

4. bMS Am 1823.4 (6).

5. bMS Am 1823.4 (7).

6. bMS Am 1823.4 (8).

7. bMS Am 1823.4 (9).

8. Ms (Cummings, EE) Works.

9. bMS Am 1823.5 (76), 'conversation with my friend is particularly'; bMS Am 1823.5 (256), 'O Thou to whom the musical white spring'; bMS Am 1823.5 (288), 'at the ferocious phenomenon of 5 o'clock' and 'perhaps it is to feel strike'.

carbon copy, probably of the typescript Cummings gave to Dos Passos. It has a title page that records the author's address as "% Morgan Harjes Co., 14 Place Vendome, Paris, France;" a complete set of poem and rubric titles; and one of the two divisional titles, "Chimneys." Each of the copy's 110 poems—the 66 published by Thomas Seltzer and 44 of the 45 published privately by the poet—is headed with a typewritten roman numeral or a carefully printed one in Cummings' hand. The pages devoted to the poems are also numbered by the poet in the upper right-hand corner. With the exception of page 116, which is omitted from the series, and the pages containing the "Sonnets—Actualities," which show signs of some last minute changes, the order of the pages and the order of the poems follow parallel courses.

The second Harvard copy is an original typescript with a carbon copy, and each of its 79 poems—43 of the 45 published by Cummings, including the poem missing from the first copy, and 36 of the 41 published by The Dial Press—is headed by a typewritten rubric as well as a roman numeral. The pages in this copy are unnumbered and five of them contain only the first line of a poem. These are the five missing texts referred to earlier. Their order in the manuscript, however, is not in doubt, for each represents the only poem in its respective sequence that is not otherwise accounted for.

Six lists confirm the overall order of the poems in the 1922 manuscript. Four of them—"Portraits," "Post Impressions," "Sonnets—Realities" and "Sonnets—Unr[ealities]"—are in the poet's hand and were found among the typescripts in the Houghton Library. The other two—"index for FORTY-ONE POEMS(the Dial Press)" and "poems not published by either Seltzer or MacVeagh,and comprised in the original Tulips & Chimneys MS"[10]—are typewritten

10. Deposit 6246-a.

and were sent to Cummings' printer and sometime publisher, S. A. Jacobs, in the spring of 1924. The typewritten lists, now in the Clifton Waller Barrett Library, University of Virginia Library, were used by Jacobs to arrange the order of the poems they identified in his 1937 *Tulips & Chimneys: Archetype Edition of the Original MS 1922.* But the listed numbering of the poems is the only thing that is "original" about the edition. The order of the 66 poems published by Seltzer was accepted without question, as were the texts of all the earlier, published versions of the poem themselves.

The 34 additional poems from *&* are arranged in the order in which Cummings published them and the texts of the poems are based on 24 typescripts in "[And] . . . Copies of the poems" and 8 individual typescripts also in the Houghton Library.[11] The poems, "suppose" and "impossibly", have been reconstructed.

With regard to the texts in general, every effort has been made to recreate the spirit as well as the letter of the originals. A few typing and spelling errors have been silently corrected and some later, published readings have been adopted but only when the poet himself was responsible for the alterations. Otherwise, the poems appear exactly as E. E. Cummings wrote them.

11. bMS Am 1823.5 (47), 'before the fragile gradual throne of night'; bMS Am 1823.5 (119), 'here is little Effie's head'; bMS Am 1823.5 (220), 'my smallheaded pearshaped'; bMS Am 1823.5 (260), 'of this sunset(which is so'; bMS Am 1823.5 (339), 'Take for example this:'; bMS Am 1823.5 (416), 'when the spent day begins to frail'; bMS Am 1892.5 (452), 'Paris;this April sunset completely utters'; bMS Am 1892.5 (566), 'the wind is a Lady with'.